BOMBER BARRON

Wing Commander James Fraser Barron
DSO & Bar, DFC, DFM, Pathfinder Pilot

RICHARD STOWERS

Richard Stowers, of Hamilton, Waikato, keenly pursues stories and original photographs of New Zealanders who were involved in local and overseas military campaigns.

Much of the inspiration for this book comes from Richard's love of New Zealand history. His father served as a bomber pilot in the Royal New Zealand Air Force, attached to the Royal Air Force, completing 42 operations and being awarded the Distinguished Flying Medal.

Other books by Richard Stowers:

Kiwi Versus Boer
Forest Rangers
The New Zealand Medal to Colonials
Rough Riders at War
Blue Devils
Bloody Gallipoli
Waikato Troopers
Cobber Kain
Von Tempsky and the Forest Rangers
Wellingtons over the Med

As with his previous books, *Bomber Barron* combines his talents of research, writing and graphic design.

Richard wishes to thank Jennifer Smith, Hugh Keane, Mark Begbie, Steve O'Toole, Matthew O'Sullivan and members of Fraser Barron's family for their enthusiasm and support in producing this book.
Photographs have come from Fraser Barron's personal albums and Rex Cording.

Copyright © Richard Stowers, 2009

First published in 2009 by Richard Stowers

rstowers@xtra.co.nz

ISBN 978-0-473-15848-4

Design by Richard Stowers

"As captain of an aircraft, Flight Lieutenant Barron has evinced a high order of courage and skill, together with determination to strike at the enemy on every possible occasion and with the greatest destructive effect. Throughout, he has given evidence of keenness and tenacity in accomplishing his allotted tasks and on many occasions has displayed a complete disregard for his personal safety."

Official Citation for Distinguished Flying Cross

A distinguished New Zealand son

Wing Commander Fraser Barron, a New Zealand airman, flew 79 bombing raids over Nazi-held Europe before he died in an aerial collision over Le Mans, France, in May 1944, just prior to the Normandy landings.

Fraser became a legend in his own lifetime. Within three years he received a 'full house' – Distinguished Service Order (DSO) and Bar, Distinguished Flying Cross (DFC) and Distinguished Flying Medal (DFM), and was promoted from Sergeant to Wing Commander. Only 55 members of the Royal New Zealand Air Force were awarded the DSO. Fraser was one of four awarded a Bar to the DSO, his being the only Bar to a New Zealander in Bomber Command. Had he lived longer, he could well have been awarded the Victoria Cross – the possibility had been spoken about.

Fraser was an outstanding bomber captain, whose skill, bravery, determination and complete disregard for his personal safety, were paramount. He was one of those young airmen who never showed fear, and didn't know when to call it quits. He became frustrated when taken off operations, bored at being an instructor, and was forever keen to get back onto front-line operations.

At the time, bomber crews were living on a knife edge – every raid was a life and death situation. As well as the horrors of flying raids, there was the waiting between them. All the dreadful scenarios for that night's operation worked on their minds. Thoughts switched to home, loved ones and friends, and eyes turned to the mess clock, watching the takeoff time draw nearer. Their fears were well founded; over 55,000 Bomber Command aircrew were killed.

Winston Churchill appropriately summed up what young men like Fraser had to endure on raids over Germany: "Night after night, month after month, our bomber squadrons travel far into Germany, find their targets in the darkness by the highest navigational skill, aim their attack often under the heaviest fire, often with serious loss, with deliberate,

"The skipper wearing battledress." The older face of Fraser after two years of operations. He is wearing the ribbons of the DSO, DFC and DFM. Below the ribbons is his Pathfinder badge. Taken in front of a Stirling at Oakington, 1943.

careful determination and inflict serious blows on the whole of the technical and war-making structure of the Nazi power. On no part of the Royal Air Force does the weight of the war fall more heavily than on the bombers."

The horrors of bombing raids, like flak and fighters, never affected Fraser. He mentally prepared himself before each operation, and took comfort in the knowledge that he was not alone with his fears. Fraser sought the companionship and trust of his own crew, always concerned about their welfare and safety. He often met them in the mess to cheerfully dissipate their private fears and doubts.

Fraser was a medium-height, black-haired and good-looking boy. He was quiet, unassuming and meticulously neat at all times. He never drank too much, and was always the perfect gentleman. He was also very popular. He flew and bombed the same way – quiet, efficient, a master at his trade.

When he arrived in England, Fraser was young and impressionable – just a boy away from home for the first time. The war quickly matured

Fraser's gallantry awards. From left: DSO with a Bar on the ribbon, DFC and DFM. They are shown in the order they are worn.

him, as it did to so many young men. However, the three long, hard years and 79 bombing operations took their toll. Towards the end he looked older than his 23 years. Because he'd been to hell and back on numerous occasions, there was a weary gauntness about his facial features.

Fraser found love before the end, meeting Marie, a young woman in the Women's Auxiliary Air Force (Waaf). As so often happened with wartime love affairs, Fraser and Marie found the strength to surmount their most unimaginable fears.

Fraser Barron was a household name and well-admired when he was alive. Yet, over 60 years later, he is largely forgotten in his homeland. Although his name and exploits were well-known amongst aircrew veterans, who frequently referred to Fraser as a hero, that generation has now largely passed on and taken their memories with them. But Fraser deserves better – he should be remembered as a national hero.

This is a story of a young man's courage, frustration, and at times, desperation. Anyone who flew 79 operations survived because they were superb pilots with accomplished crews – and unbelievably lucky!

Unfortunately, in May 1944, the odds finally turned against Fraser.

Small beginnings

James Fraser Barron was born in Dunedin on 9 January 1921. Fraser's father, James, was a grocer and during the late 1920s purchased a store in Maheno, just south of Oamaru. Fraser had an older sister, Patsy, and the family lived in a large, rambling house at the rear of the store. His first school was the Maheno Primary School.

At the start of 1934 Fraser became a student at Waitaki Boys' High School in Oamaru. The total school roll at the time was about 430, a large step-up for a young rural boy. He travelled daily to and from the school by train from Maheno. When the Barron family sold

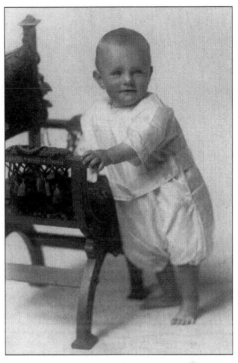

Fraser as a baby. A relative has humorously titled the reverse of the photograph, "Fraser Barron, DSO & Bar, DFC, DFM."

up at Maheno in June of the same year, they shifted to Fairlie township in South Canterbury, about 40 miles inland from Timaru. Fraser became a boarder at Waitaki Boys' High, returning home most weekends and for holidays.

At school he loved rugby and at just five feet six inches in height and of slight build, was one of the school's lightest players to take the field. Fraser also had a keen interest in athletics, cricket and tennis.

Students at Fraser's school became increasingly concerned about the possibility of another world war. This was reflected in topics chosen for school debates and essay writing. Aviation, too, became a favourite

Top: "My mother and father," James and Winifred Ellen (nee Fraser) Barron.

Below: The Barron residence, Fairlie, Canterbury.

subject for many of the boys.

It is not known exactly when Fraser was lured to aviation. Kingsford Smith flying the *Southern Cross* visited New Zealand in 1933, and flew the length of the country, stopping at places along the way. To fund his adventures he offered rides at a nominal price and Fraser was one of the boys who talked his father into paying for a flight. When Fraser arrived back on the ground, a friend at the time said, "he was delighted with the experience."

A fictional story titled 'Clipped wings,' that was printed in the school magazine, has been attributed to Fraser. The story tells of a pilot who lost his legs in a crash but wanted to continue flying. It was a young boy's fantasy of high adventure and dashing heroics in aeroplanes.

Fraser repeated his imaginative writing skills in an essay written the same year. The theme again was aviation. With fanciful foresight, Fraser mentioned such things as searchlights flashing about the sky, dull booms and aerial attacks. There is a cry of, "The country has been attacked from the air, without the declaration of war!" Young Fraser didn't realise how foreboding his thoughts were.

At the end of 1937 Fraser left Waitaki Boys' High after successfully passing all the mandatory exams of the time. He was considered an average academic student. By early 1938 he was working as a clerical cadet in the Mines Department in Wellington, where he boarded at the YMCA and played rugby for the Wellington Football Club.

After war was declared in Europe during September 1939, Fraser

"Dad with Fraser." Defence Rifle Club gathering. Fraser, in school uniform, is sitting on his father's lap.

wasted no time in volunteering for aircrew training. Still aged 18 years, he made his first application on 5 October. Although parental approval was needed for those under 21 before they could proceed overseas, young Fraser was not daunted by the prospect of not getting his parents' consent. Once he had completed his prerequisite course, he had to sit back and wait.

Fraser's call-up finally came through requiring him to report to RNZAF (Royal New Zealand Air Force) Station Levin (Wereroa) on 2 July 1940. The final selection for training as a pilot, observer, or air gunner, would depend on the results obtained from the four-week course. On 24 June, Fraser's training prospects were thrown into confusion when he received another training offer with the Fleet Air Arm with the chance of an early commission, provided he was prepared to leave for England in just three weeks.

To go, Fraser needed parental consent. Expecting to receive his parents' approval, Fraser, with a group of about 20 others, reported for a pre-admission interview. All the group, including Fraser, confirmed they were available to depart overseas, but later in the day a telegram arrived from his mother declining permission. Fraser was disappointed. He wrote, "I was very sorry you couldn't see eye to eye with me over this chance I got yesterday. It was a wonderful chance and had you known more about it I am sure you would have agreed to it. I don't suppose I'll ever get the same chance again … I was always very keen about getting a commission."

On the morning of 2 July, with a group of about 100 others, Fraser reported to Ground Training School at RNZAF Station Levin. He was now NZ401749 LAC (Leading Aircraftman) James Fraser Barron.

Fraser (2nd from right) as a harem dancer in a school concert at Waitaki Boys' High School.

Fraser (front, 2nd from left) played rugby for the Wellington Football Club during the winter of 1938.

Fraser (in centre with binoculars) and friends watch an air display at Rongotai aerodrome, Wellington, 1938.

Fraser (front) at a tennis party, 1939.

Learning to fly

"Walking in" to Levin Ground Training School, Fraser was first kitted out, receiving an oversized uniform which forced him to visit the station tailor for some necessary alterations. He was also issued with a flying helmet, goggles, Gosport speaking tubes and gauntlets. But the clothing store had no size 6 flying boots.

Levin was a basic training facility, where new recruits spent most of their time on the parade ground or in the classroom. To Fraser, there seemed to be an endless amount of discipline and saluting. With all the examinations successfully behind him, he left Levin on 27 July 1940, crossing from Wellington to Lyttelton by inter-island steamer the same night.

Fraser reached Taieri, near Dunedin, on 29 July to commence his training on aircraft at No. 1 Elementary Flying Training School (EFTS). He joined Course 3A and shared it with Jimmy Ward, later to be awarded the Victoria Cross, and Jim Starky, later a highly-decorated Squadron Leader. The three became close friends. "We started flying the same day we got here much to our surprise. Since then we have been flying every

Members of Course 3A at Taieri, 1940. Fraser is front right, with friend Jimmy Ward 2nd from right in the back row.

day except Friday when it was too rough." Fraser's instructor was Flying Officer LF Poore for whom Barron developed a great admiration. "He is one of the two best instructors here so I was lucky to get him. There are four of us to each instructor. We fly twice one day and once the next."

According to Fraser, the pace at Taieri was "slack" compared to Levin. "There is very little drill and we are left to ourselves quite a bit. The officers are a decent lot and help us all they can. They don't seem to worry whether we salute them or not."

Fraser spent his time at Taieri on Tiger Moths and believed them to be "almost perfectly safe." He reckoned that if

Fraser while at Taieri, 1940. Behind him is a Tiger Moth training aircraft.

anything went wrong, all you had to do was take your hands off the controls and the aircraft righted itself.

For the trainee pilots, the best aspect about Taieri was they had Wednesday, Friday and Saturday nights and all day Sunday off. Free time spent off the base was mostly taken up shopping and going to the pictures in Dunedin.

Before a trainee pilot could go solo, he was required to have instruction in how to control spinning. The very day Fraser had this instruction, he ate a hearty breakfast. "As the sun was bad for practising landings the instructor decided to do spinning which is compulsory for every pupil before going solo. Spinning is an aerobatic manoeuvre and is done by putting the nose down and spinning down. We went up to 4000 feet and did four spins. That turned me up a bit and then he asked me if I'd like to do a loop and a slow roll. I said yes and he did it." When they landed

Publicity photograph taken at Wigram, 1940. Fraser is 3rd from right.

Fraser walked over to the hangar and was sick. The instructor laughed and said not to worry as everyone did it.

It seems Fraser was quick to learn flying solo. "I went solo on Friday after nine and three quarter hours, so they didn't waste much time … I didn't think he [the instructor] was going to pass me because he made me do five circuits and landings with him for the test. However, at the end of the test he took me back to the hangar and got out and told me to do one circuit on my own. I got around alright except that I didn't allow for the plane being lighter without the instructor and by the time I got back to the aerodrome I was too high to land, so I went round again."

Fraser got in fine this time after a bumpy landing. "When I taxied back to the hangar and got out, my instructor came over and shook hands. I was the first of his pupils to go solo." Fraser flew solo on 9 August.

Apparently, no one was allowed to fly solo unless they had completed at least eight hours dual. If anyone took more than 15 hours they were kicked out of pilot training.

The following day, after a circuit and landing with the instructor aboard, Fraser did three circuits and landings on his own, and was about to climb from the aircraft when he was told to do three more. Over the following weeks Fraser became a proficient pilot. Then it was time to move on.

Course 3A, including Fraser, shifted from Taieri to No. 1 Flying Training School (FTS) at Wigram, outside Christchurch, on 28 September.

"I am flying Fairey Gordons. They are very different from a Tiger Moth as they are about four times as big and are very heavy on the controls, but I like them better each time."

While at Wigram, fellow trainee Basil Sharp and Fraser purchased a wireless set for £4. "We put in £2 each and it is well worth it. It is a six-valve Philco and has a very good tone. We can get Australia on it. We got it on Friday night and have had it going flat out ever since." The radio helped the young pilots to relax by filling their accommodation quarters with the latest dance music. However, it was not long before rain got into the radio and they had to wait for a station wireless operator to fix it.

Another test for pilot training was the altitude test. "I had to do my altitude test last Monday morning. I went up to 16,000 feet and stayed there for half an hour. I was pretty fed up by the time I finished as all I

Publicity photograph in front of an Oxford aircraft, Wigram 1940. Fraser is in the centre.

(l-r): Rowland, AM Wackman and Fraser. Wigram, 1940.

Fraser (centre) and mates escape to the beach in an RNZAF ambulance.

A line-up of Gordons at Wigram, 1940.

A Gordon prepares for takeoff.

Fraser adjusts his harness before a flight in a Gordon.

had to do was to fly back and forward. I made one mistake – it was dinner time when time was up, and being in a hurry I dived down most of the way instead of taking it easy." The result was that Fraser's ears were blocked and he walked around near-deaf for a couple of days, much to the amusement of his colleagues.

But Fraser managed to have some laughs at the expense of others. One day the wind switched quickly to the opposite direction. "There were a lot of planes up and they didn't notice the change. Four planes tried to land downwind, the wrong way. The whole station was out to watch them and it was as good as a play to see them land, and not being able to stop. They had to take off again or they would have run into the fence at 100mph." Fortunately they all woke up to it in time and approached upwind.

Another milestone in pilot proficiency was to take up a passenger for the first time. It seems the ground staff were picked on for guinea pigs. "On Friday morning I took up my first passenger. We had to take up a passenger before we could get our wings. I took up one of the ground

Fraser (centre) and others pose for a publicity photograph. Wigram 1940.

staff chaps and he seemed quite keen about going. It wasn't a very good day for it but I got him back in one piece and he thanked me."

It seems that some instructors had a bent for aerobatics. On one occasion Fraser was up with an instructor in a light aircraft doing some blind flying when he "was taught how to loop-the-loop."

One Friday the Governor General visited Wigram. The trainees did a march past followed by an aerobatic and dive-bombing display put on by the instructors.

A cameraman filmed the trainees marching and doing a mock scramble. "A Movietone cameraman filmed us as we marched past and in the afternoon we had to dress up in our flying gear and run out and man the planes while the cameraman filmed us. So far, none of us has had a contract from Hollywood!"

Fraser had now reached the stage of training when cross-country flights became a regular thing. "We will be doing a few cross-country trips next week. I did my first last Thursday with the instructor. It was a triangular course, Wigram – Hororata – Oxford – Wigram." Other flights took him on courses over both north and south Canterbury and as far afield as Blenheim and Taieri. Once they flew over the Southern Alps at 8000 feet to Hokitika and back. "When we got over to the West Coast it was cloudy so we didn't see Hokitika."

On New Year's Day 1941, Fraser and another trainee pilot flew from Wigram to Taieri on a cross-country flight. They followed the coastline south. "It was quite a good day over Canterbury and we could see a crowd of people on the beach at Timaru. We went down and waved to them. In the afternoon we were to go on the same trip changing pilots, but we refused as we had been there three times, so they sent us to Lake Heron and Geraldine."

Training at Wigram included Armament Camp, which involved dropping practice bombs on targets. The camp proved a new experience for both pilots and instructors. "It was a lot of fun while it lasted. We are the first course to do dive bombing here and the planes aren't much good for it so all the instructors were waiting to see the results. The first chap put all his bombs about 600 yards away from the target and the second chap put his first bomb nearly a mile away!

"I was third to try but after I dropped three bombs the bomb-release

(l-r): R Taylor, JG Grant, WR Culpan, R Miller, GK Williams, Rowland, AM Wackman and Fraser. Wigram 1940.

Publicity photograph taken at Wigram, 1940. Fraser is 2nd from right. They were issued new flying suits for the occasion.

jammed and I had to come home." Fraser's three bombs were only slightly closer to the target.

The next day the instructor went up and experimented for himself. He then took the trainee pilots up one at a time, demonstrating the corrected method. Before long they were dropping their bombs within 100 yards of the target. "I have hit the target once and some of the boys hit it two or three times." The following week they practised low-level bombing.

Wigram was not always suitable for flying as fog and low cloud often sat over the station. On the first flyable day after a week of such conditions, eight trainees, including Fraser, and an instructor flew out to Banks Peninsula and landed in a paddock beside the sea. Another instructor flew a target-towing aircraft overhead and the trainees spent the day firing at the target with camera guns. They also chased the target aircraft in the air over the sea attacking it from behind. "When we weren't flying we did some sunbathing. It was just like a picnic."

Another weather condition that hampered flying over Canterbury was the "nor'wester," because most of the training aircraft at Wigram were light and handling them was difficult in strong winds. "Next week, with the exception of Mondays, we have to start getting up at 4 o'clock in the mornings. It is always done here in summer in order to dodge the northwest winds. The [flying] day will finish for us at two o'clock in the afternoon."

Fraser received his Pilot's Badge or 'wings' on 12 December 1940, and was promoted to sergeant on 18 January 1941, the day he graduated from the course. At midday he caught the southbound express, arriving at Palmerston, north of Dunedin, that evening. His parents had moved there recently. After saying all his final goodbyes, he headed

The young face of Sergeant Fraser Barron, after graduation and presentation of "wings," January 1941.

north by train on 25 January to catch the inter-island steamer that night to Wellington. From there Fraser travelled by overnight express to Auckland arriving at 5am on 27 January. En route, his sister Patsy

Fraser (2nd from left) and others in front of a Gordon aircraft, Wigram 1940.

Fraser (left) with sister Patsy and Jimmy Ward. Auckland, January 1941.

boarded the train at Te Kuiti. Patsy stayed with Fraser and Jimmy Ward before the two airmen and other members of Course 3A joined the *Aorangi* on 29 January. When Patsy said goodbye, she presented Fraser with a greenstone tiki which he wore on every raid.

As Fraser's war progressed, he became a regular letter writer, mostly to his mother and sister Patsy. Fortunately, enough of them survive today to string together a sequence of events, and to reveal his thoughts and emotions at the time. Maybe Fraser was following the wishes of his mother, as he wrote home most Sundays. If he missed a week or day, there was usually an apology and an explanation at the start of the next letter. Nearly all of Fraser's quotes in this book are taken from these 'time capsule' letters. Further quotes are taken from his log book, wartime interviews and newspaper articles.

Off to war

Fraser left Auckland aboard the *Aorangi* of the Canadian Australasian Line, at 11.15am on 30 January 1941. "We came aboard yesterday afternoon and slept aboard. The sergeant pilots are travelling first class and our cabins are very comfortable ... We had our last shore leave last night and we went to the pictures. We had to be back on the ship by midnight. This morning we had our first meal on the ship and it was pretty good, just like a first-class hotel.

"The ship is carrying nearly all Air Force men. There are 200 Australians going to Canada and the New Zealanders are 40 observers, 20 gunners and about 30 sergeant pilots and pilot officers."

Their first port of call was Suva, Fiji, where with a couple of mates, Fraser went ashore for a few hours. They visited a friend who was stationed at an army camp situated about three miles from Suva. Afterwards, they shopped in Suva, and Fraser purchased a sun helmet and a silver chain for his greenstone tiki. He was pleased to get back on board because "there are so few cars there that the drivers take the corners

Fraser (centre) shopping in Suva. Included in his purchases was a silver chain for his greenstone tiki.

at 60 miles per hour and there seems to be no traffic rules at all!" They left Suva at 10 that evening.

The men struggled with the high temperatures while crossing the tropics. "There wasn't a cool spot on the ship. I couldn't even sit down to read without sweat running off me in a stream. At the pictures at night all the boys would wear was a pair of shorts." A large canvas tank on the top deck filled with seawater proved very popular with the men.

On the Aorangi, this large canvas "pool" on the top deck proved very popular with the men.

Their last port of call was Victoria on Vancouver Island, before they berthed at Vancouver on 16 February, where the New Zealanders disembarked and climbed aboard a train for a five-day trans-continental ride to the Atlantic. They were greeted at every stop across Canada, but "the best reception we got was at Winnipeg. A big crowd came to see us and

Fraser and Jimmy Ward keep warm in Canada.

when we marched into the station everybody cheered. Some society gave us magazines, chocolate and cigarettes." The men needed cheering as the outside temperature was -30 degrees Fahrenheit. At the small town of Truro, about 60 miles from Halifax, Nova Scotia, the contingent halted for a couple of days before embarking for Britain on 23 February. Fraser sailed from Halifax aboard the Cunard White Star Liner *Georgic*. Conditions on the ship were a little more crowded than on the *Aorangi*, as he now shared his cabin with three others.

The *Georgic* didn't travel in convoy and sped across the Atlantic arriving at Liverpool, England, on 5 March. From there the New Zealand contingent boarded a train and departed for RAF (Royal Air Force) Uxbridge, 18 miles west of London.

At Uxbridge forms were completed and identification cards and equipment issued. Each man received £14 which, Fraser noted, "Came in very handy". Finally on 9 March, the Airmen Pilots' Course 3A were given their postings. It was to be their first separation since they started training at Levin in July of the previous year.

Fraser was posted to heavy bombers. Three of those to accompany Fraser to 20 Bomber OTU (Operational Training Unit) at RAF Lossiemouth, Scotland, were friends Jim Starky, Jimmy Ward and Johnny Culpan. Others went to Fighter and Coastal Commands.

The Lossiemouth-bound group left Kings Cross Station in London at 5pm, 10 March. Once at Lossiemouth, in the north of Scotland, Fraser trained blind flying on a Link Trainer, an early flight simulator. He was one of about 40 New Zealand pilots stationed at Lossiemouth. In the evenings he and others would go to the pictures after a large supper.

A Wellington bomber, similar to those flown by Fraser at Lossiemouth.

Fraser commented, "The New Zealanders are very popular up here in Scotland. The Aussies and Canadians don't get much of a hearing but we get a good time."

Fraser was converting to twin-engined aircraft and his first bomber, the Vickers Wellington. "I had a good look inside one the other day and they look pretty good to me, and safe as a bank."

While in Scotland Fraser was fitted out for a kilt which took seven yards of material at a total cost of £6. Rugby was never far from the mind of a serving New Zealander, and it wasn't long before "we are thinking of getting up a New Zealand rugby football team to take on the Royal Engineers, and anyone else who cares for a game."

Vickers Wellington

The Wellington, affectionately known as the "Wimpey," proved to be the mainstay of Bomber Command throughout the first three years of the war.

The first unit to receive the Wellington Mk I was 99 Squadron based at RAF Mildenhall in October 1938, and by September 1939 a further seven squadrons had converted to Wellingtons.

Designed by Barnes Wallis using geodetic construction, the Wellington proved to be a sturdy aircraft, with a total of 11,461 being manufactured.

At the commencement of hostilities, Wellingtons were principally involved in daytime operations, but as raids were flown against increasing fighter opposition, their role was switched to nighttime.

The Wellington's capacious bomb bay also meant that it could carry 2000-pound, and later 4000-pound, bombs.

The final Wellington version to see service with Bomber Command was the Mark X which was introduced in late 1942. Wellingtons also saw active service in the Middle and Far East as well as at home with Coastal Command.

The peak of the Wellington's service probably came in 1942, when just over half of the forces of the three 1000-bomber raids were Wellingtons.

Specifications (Mk III)

Length:	60ft 10in (18.54m)
Wingspan:	86ft 2in (26.25m)
Maximum speed:	255mph (411kph)
Cruising speed:	180mph (290kph)
Ceiling:	18,000ft (5484m)
Range:	1540 miles (2484km) with 4500lb (2043kg) bomb-load
Engines:	Two Bristol Hercules XI of 1500hp each
Payload:	4500lbs (2043kg)
Armament:	2 x .303 machine guns in nose and 4 in tail turret
Crew:	5

In Scotland, Fraser was able to buy a kilt in his family's Fraser tartan. Lossiemouth, 1941.

After completing part of their course at Lossiemouth, Fraser and others went on leave. The RAF gave them free rail passes to anywhere in Britain; three men went to London but most decided to go to Edinburgh.

"We got to Edinburgh at 9.15pm in the middle of a blackout and a snowstorm, so we took a taxi to the Grosvenor Hotel which had been recommended to us. They charged 10s/6d per day including all meals so we decided to stay. Jim Starky, Johnny Culpan and I got a room together and it was very comfortable. We even had a telephone."

The meals were great and there was plenty to eat, although sugar and butter were a bit short. They managed to take in the sights and went to a show, and of course – to the pictures. And after tea they went to the pictures again!

On his return to Lossiemouth, Fraser stopped at Aberdeen for a few days, only to be stricken with illness. "I am writing this in the Aberdeen Hospital where I have been for nearly three weeks. On the last day of leave I was taken to the hospital with scarlet fever, and last week on the day I was due to get up, I developed the measles."

While Fraser was in hospital, a single German raider came over and dropped two bombs about two hundred yards away, aiming at the nearby gasworks. "They went right over the hospital at about 100 feet and we could feel the bombs shake the ward."

As a result of the illness, on his eventual return to Lossiemouth, Fraser was put back several flying courses. It was some time since he had last piloted an aircraft – 16 January to be precise – over three months previously.

Fraser returned to new accommodation situated about a mile from the base. The billet was a large house built like a miniature castle. Although five men shared his room, it proved very comfortable. "Between us we have got two wireless sets, a gramophone, a bagpipe chanter and a ukulele, so there is always plenty of noise."

Fraser started flying again on 19 May, when he did two hours of dual flying in a Wellington with a sergeant instructor. "I found the Wellington a bit strange after flying Gordons at home but after a couple of hours on Friday I am getting the idea. They are great planes to fly. They are just like a house inside and are very comfortable."

At the beginning of June, Fraser wrote home, "By jove, we have been busy. We have been put into what is known as Operational Flight to do cross-country flights, and we were also put into crews. Over the next fortnight we worked harder than any of us had ever done before. We flew nearly every day and night and in one week I did nearly 50 hours' flying. It took me eight weeks to do that much when I was at Taieri. All we did was sleep and fly, and eat when we could."

On the night of 17/18 June, Fraser had the unnerving experience of ditching an aircraft in the sea. The crew took off during darkness on a cross-country navigation exercise. About 40 miles from Lossiemouth, out over the North Sea, trouble developed in one of the engines and it had to be shut down. As a result they lost height quickly and soon realised they wouldn't reach the aerodrome at Lossiemouth. Rather than risk an uncontrolled crash-landing in darkness, Fraser decided to ditch as close as possible to shore, realising that shallow water was the safer option. At 3.15am they finally hit the water about 40 yards from shore and "everybody got out O.K."

While stationed at Lossiemouth Fraser completed 35 conversion flights on Wellingtons – 18 of these as pilot. Flying time totalled just under 80 hours. During that time he was made first pilot and captain of his crew. "It may sound alright being captain, but it meant a bit of extra work and responsibility." Fraser's crew was a league of nations, "a Canadian, an Englishman, a Welshman, a Scotsman, a white chap from Malaya and myself, a New Zealander."

Don Hodge, Fraser's friend and son of Mrs Ireland, was killed on 1 September 1941.

Training flights took them over some of the more beautiful regions of Scotland. "We were over among the Western Isles of Scotland and as we had a clear sky and ideal conditions, it was a wonderful sight. The calm, deep blue sea and the wild Scottish west coast is something I'll never forget. We passed over the very heart of the Highlands. I could see very few roads, but plenty of hills and lochs … I could see some old ruins and the outline of churches and other buildings which must have been there for hundreds of years."

Fraser graduated from Lossiemouth on 24 June. Before his next appointment, he spent fives days' leave with Don Hodge, another pilot he shared the course with. They visited Don's family home in Westmorland in the middle of the Lake District, having a wonderful time. "We were staying in a village called Ambleside, which is on the shores of Lake Windermere, and we did quite a lot of rowing and fishing on the lake." Don's mother had re-married Mr Ireland, and their home would become Fraser's 'home away from home' while serving in the Air Force. Mrs Ireland "has asked me to make my home there while I am over here and I am to go there for my leave whenever I get it."

Getting down to business

On 24 June 1941 Fraser reported to 15 Squadron at Wyton, outside Huntingdon in Cambridgeshire, about 60 miles north of London. At Wyton, "We are going onto one of the biggest and latest bombers in the world. It is the Stirling and has four engines." One could hardly say that Fraser was ready for the change to four engines. Of the 80 hours he flew on Wellingtons at Lossiemouth, he'd only completed 19:05 hours of day and 14:30 hours of night flying as first pilot. But there was a reason for the shortfall – due to the limited number of Stirlings produced to date, no Heavy Conversion Unit (HCU) had been established with these aircraft. This meant that Fraser had to do his conversion training with the new squadron.

"But believe me it's a wonderful machine." Neither the marked swing to starboard on take-off, slow rate of climb, limited ceiling, high-nose attitude during landing on the gangling undercarriage, nor the problems with the Exactor controls for the throttles, would appear to have discouraged Fraser. He knew better than to divulge too many technical details in his letters. Fraser didn't know that only eight conversion flights

Stirling 3665, flown by Fraser in a raid to Brest on the night of 3/4 September 1941. The aircraft lacks the large LS squadron markings on the fuselage, indicating this photograph was probably taken soon after its delivery to 15 Squadron.

29

over five days on Stirlings lay between then and his first raid on Germany just two weeks later, on the night of 7/8 July. For all eight flights, Fraser acted as second pilot to Flight Lieutenant Best.

15 Squadron was only the second Bomber Command squadron to be equipped with the giant Short Stirling, the first example reaching the unit on 11 April 1941. Fraser considered himself lucky to be put on Stirlings, as Bomber Command was putting experienced crews on the new type first. This may be the first indication that Fraser was considered

Short Stirling

The Stirling was the first four-engined bomber to serve with the RAF. Air Ministry specifications restricted its wingspan to no more than 100 feet to enable the aircraft to fit inside some current RAF hangars. As a consequence, the Stirling's performance suffered, as the wings could not generate the lift required to operate at high altitudes when carrying a full load.

Stirling Mk Is flew their maiden operation on the night of 10/11 February 1941.

But by then it was apparent that the lack of power produced by the four Bristol engines severely limited the load-carrying ability of the Stirling.

On operations against long-range targets such as Italy or deep inside Germany, the Stirling was restricted to just 3500 pounds of bombs and could barely climb over the Alps during flights to and from Italy. In addition, the narrow design of the bomb bay restricted the carrying of large, single bombs.

To help overcome some of these limitations, the Mk III was introduced from the start of 1943. But still the aircraft suffered much higher losses than other aircraft of the Main Force. Within five months of being introduced, 67 out of the 84 aircraft delivered had been lost to enemy action or written off after crashes. Most of these were attributed to the Stirling's low ceiling making it more vulnerable to flak. As a result, during 1943 Stirlings were gradually phased out of the Main Force and used as minelayers, troop carriers or glider tugs, being used during D-Day operations. Their final Bomber Command operation was flown on 8 September 1944.

In all, the Stirling dropped only 27,821 tons of bombs, compared to 41,800 for the Wellington, 227,000 for the Halifax and 608,612 for the Lancaster. However, it was also responsible for dropping 20,000 mines into German-controlled waters.

Excluding the Mk V transport variant, 2221 were delivered to the RAF.

Specifications (Mk III)

Length:	87ft 3in (26.58m)
Wingspan:	99ft 1in (30.19m)
Maximum speed:	270mph (435kph)
Cruising speed:	200mph (323kph)
Ceiling:	17,500ft (5332m)
Range:	2010 miles (3242km) with 3500lb (1589kg) bomb-load
Engines:	Four Bristol Hercules XVIs of 1650hp each
Payload:	14,000lbs (6356kg)
Armament:	2 x .303 machine guns in nose and mid-upper turrets, and 4 in tail turret
Crew:	7

to be a superior pilot by senior officers – a quick promotion to 'heavies' seemed inevitable.

The new station soon got Fraser's approval. "The sergeants' mess is very comfortable and the food is pretty good." At the time there were about six New Zealanders in the Squadron. Fraser's new instructor, Flight Lieutenant Best, was a Kiwi. Fraser thought him a great chap who spoke his mind in plain language.

Fraser adapted very quickly to the Stirling. "These new planes are great and I am having no trouble in flying them. If we land at another aerodrome we are always objects of envy and admiration."

Because of all the flat country around Wyton,

Flying Officer Peter Boggis about to enter Stirling N6030. Fraser completed his first two operations in this aircraft during July 1941, with Boggis captaining the first, a raid on Frankfurt.

Fraser and his crew had trouble locating the airfield from the air, "as all the fields look exactly alike to me. Every time I go up I lose the aerodrome and it takes me quite a time to find it again."

Fraser's first operation took place on the night of 7/8 July, in a small raid on Frankfurt by three Stirlings from 15 Squadron and 14 Halifaxes. Fraser was second pilot to Flying Officer Peter Boggis. The three Stirlings together dropped fifteen 1000-pounders and twenty-five 500-pounders, plus a quantity of incendiaries. It would appear, however, that Boggis' bomb-load was dropped over Hochheim, 15 miles to the

An action shot of a 15 Squadron Stirling flying through flak, snapped from an accompanying Stirling on a Circus raid into France, 1941.

west of Frankfurt. The operation took 5:15 hours. One Halifax was lost.

Boggis usually flew 'MacRobert's Reply,' an aircraft gifted by Lady Rachael MacRobert in memory of her three sons killed while flying – one was killed in a pre-war civil flying accident, and the other two killed in 1941 while serving with the RAF.

The main raids on the night were to Cologne, Osnabrück, Münster and Mönchengladbach, involving 181 Wellingtons, 54 Whitleys and 40 Hampdens.

On the same night, for his gallantry while returning from Münster, Sergeant Jimmy Ward of 75 New Zealand Squadron, was awarded the Victoria Cross. Jimmy had trained alongside Fraser both in New Zealand and at 20 OTU, Lossiemouth.

The Stirling was briefly used by Bomber Command on daylight *Circus* operations during the summer of 1941. These raids into occupied Europe were designed to force the Luftwaffe to retaliate, as earlier fighter sweeps without bombers had been ignored by the Luftwaffe. The Stirling was not an ideal aircraft for these missions – in one month of *Circus* operations

Stirlings of 15 Squadron flanked by Hurricane fighters, on a daylight Circus raid into France, 1941.

five would be lost and 11 damaged, mostly by anti-aircraft fire. It was realised that these raids were a waste of the new four-engined heavies, and the Stirlings in this role were quickly replaced by twin-engined bombers.

2 Three Stirlings of 15 Squadron turned to daylight duties on 9 July with a raid on Mazingarbe, close to Béthune, northern France. Fraser was second pilot to the Squadron Leader, Wing Commander Ogilvie. The primary target was the synthetic oil plant at Mazingarbe, but the target couldn't be located because of thick haze in the target area. The official report stated, "Owing to haze up to 6000 feet, [Labuissière aerodrome at Béthune] was bombed by mistake." The 15 Squadron Operational Record Book said that a factory was attacked at Labuissière but "the bombs unfortunately overshot the mark." The Channel-hop operation took exactly three hours.

A contemporary newspaper article goes some way to describe the raid. "13-8 IN DAY AIR SWOOP: Heavy bombers of the RAF, escorted by fighters, made a daring daylight raid yesterday on a power station near

33

Béthune, northern France. The target was hit by heavy bombs. During the operation 13 enemy fighters were destroyed, one by a bomber and 12 by the escort. Eight of our fighters are missing, but the pilot of one is safe."

3 The squadron took part in a further daylight raid just two days later, with Fraser as second pilot to Boggis. Fraser's aircraft bombed Hazebrouck on 11 July, taking 3:25 hours to complete the operation. The primary target was Fives-Lille steel and engineering works in the city of Lille, but a thunderstorm over the target prevented it being located. Instead, marshalling yards at Hazebrouck were selected. According to the Operational Record Book, "Direct hits were obtained by at least two of the three sticks on the yards and the station was also badly hit." In total, six Stirlings attacked both Hazebrouck and Le Trait shipyard in what were termed 'minor ops'.

Over the next two days Fraser took part in two minor daylight raids, the first destined for St Omer, France, inland from Calais. Both missions

A 15 Squadron Stirling crew walking in line for the camera. Flying Officer Boggis, captain, is wearing the white flying suit with Fraser, second pilot, to his left. This is possibly the crew of Fraser's very first operation to Frankfurt on the night of 7/8 July 1941.

Ground crew swarm over a Stirling while petrol and oil are supplied. Even before a target is known, the petrol load gave crews some indication of the likely distance involved.

were abandoned in the air – possibly because heavy cloud obscured the targets – and were not included in Fraser's tally of operations. The St Omer operation still managed to clock up 2:55 hours.

4 On 18 July Fraser returned to Germany in an ambitious cloud-covered daylight raid on the Ruhr. Again he acted as second pilot to Boggis. Five Stirlings took part with one being lost in the sea. This raid, too, was turned back, but with a total flight time of just two hours – it was still added to Fraser's tally. The heavy Stirling was proving unsuitable for daylight raids. Perhaps Bomber Command was finally learning that un-escorted bombers were extremely vulnerable during daytime missions.

Fraser went on leave after the attempted raid on the Ruhr. He took the opportunity to revisit Mr and Mrs Caie, a family that befriended him when he was a patient in Aberdeen Hospital. The weather was not the best but he managed to have a "good time and a good rest".

5 One week later on 25 July, again as second pilot to Boggis, Fraser flew on a nighttime raid to Berlin but ended up bombing the alternative target of Münster. The flight took 4:35 hours. Seven Stirlings

and two Halifaxes took part in the minor operation, with two Stirlings and one Halifax being lost, an astounding one third of the force.

About this time Fraser was invited to have tea at an old English manor house near Wyton. He found the house and his hosts "so typical. The people, although very kind, were book-perfect down to the last detail, and I was on pins and needles all the time in case I did or said something which wasn't in keeping with best society. I'm afraid they were a bit above me socially." Fraser must have come across to them as a brusque colonial boy from the far-off Antipodes. "There was a marked silence once when a lady asked me what kind of music I liked and I said bagpipes and 'swing'. I found out afterwards that Handel and Beethoven were their idea of music."

6 Fraser's next operation took him to Berlin on the night of 2/3 August. Again Fraser was second pilot to Boggis. Only five Stirlings took part in the operation, out of a total of 53 aircraft. One Stirling was lost. After Fraser's longest flight yet of 6:35 hours, they had to land at Honnington due to heavy fog at Wyton. Over the following week Fraser and his crew practised blind approaches on a dozen occasions in the hope of making them more prepared for fog in the future.

7 On the night of 5/6 August a flight of 6:25 hours took Fraser and his crew to the distant city of Karlsruhe. Again Boggis was captain and Fraser the second pilot. A total of 97 aircraft took part, eight of them Stirlings, with three aircraft being lost. Their mission was to hit railway targets, but German reports indicate these were largely missed.

8 Fraser's next operation was a daring single-bomber raid on the marshalling yards at Bielefeld on the night of 12/13 August. For this special low-level raid of 6:15 hours, Wing Commander Ogilvie was in command and Fraser was second pilot. Ogilvie had come up with the idea of a nighttime low-level attack against a target of opportunity, using a Stirling. Authority was granted to him by the commanding officer of 3 Bomber Group, indicative of the 'learn by experience' attitude of Bomber Command at the time.

A contemporary newspaper article stated, "A Stirling crossed the coast

Photograph snapped from a cockpit of Stirlings flying in formation over Britain.

at 400 feet and then cruised round the Ruhr mostly at 300 feet and never above 1000 feet. The pilot finally found a good target and dropped his load of bombs [from 800 feet]."

To Fraser the operation must have had all the elements of a *Boy's Own Annual,* as he excitedly wrote home some weeks later, "Don't know whether you heard about a Stirling crossing the Dutch coast and coming through the Ruhr at 300 feet, but I was in it. I was a second pilot then and our commanding officer, a wing commander, was captain. It was the most exciting trip I've been on. At times we were down as low as factory chimneys and our machine was riddled with bullet holes." This was probably not what his mother wanted to read.

Apparently, on reaching the target area, the bomb aimer couldn't sight their objective owing to bad visibility, and as it was too dangerous to hang around at such low altitude, Ogilvie opted to bomb their alternative target down the Ruhr. Fraser later said, "The explosion nearly blew us out of the sky. It was terrific!" In doing so, the Stirling had to run the gauntlet of murderous light flak for some time, and probably survived because the Germans weren't expecting an attack at such a low level and because Ogilvie worked hard at keeping beneath the incoming tracer. It was a wonder that no crew member or vital aircraft component was hit.

Amazingly, the large, lumbering Stirling bomber was being used in the same role as the high-performance Mosquitoes were used later in the war. Surely this must rate as one of the more daring air operations of the Second World War.

On 15 August Fraser took leave again. This time he stayed with Mr and Mrs Ireland in Ambleside. Because of his early morning arrival after a night on the train, he was given breakfast and then slept until late afternoon. The following day "it was raining and I stayed in bed until dinnertime."

9 On the night of 25/26 August Fraser returned to Karlsruhe as second pilot with Boggis as captain. The flight took 5:40 hours with 12 Stirlings and 37 other aircraft participating. Storms and thick cloud prevented accurate bombing, and three aircraft were lost, including one Stirling.

10 Fraser's tenth operation was his last as second pilot. As on seven of Fraser's previous raids, Boggis was captain. The target was railways in Duisburg and took 4:15 hours on the night of 28/29 August. 118 bombers took part including 13 Stirlings. To date, this was the most Stirlings on any raid, indicating that squadron numbers of the type were slowly increasing. Six aircraft were lost including one Stirling. Good bombing was claimed in clear visibility, but Duisburg later reported only 63 high-explosive and 500 incendiary bombs hitting the city.

In the driver's seat

On 1 September 1941 Fraser was promoted to flight sergeant and became captain of his own aircraft and crew. "Last week I was made a captain and I have got my own crew now. They are a good lot of chaps in the crew and we have a pretty good time together. One of them, the new gunner, was in my crew when we were in Scotland."

Sadly, Don Hodge, Fraser's friend and son of Mrs Ireland, was killed on 1 September. His bomber was coming in to land at night when it was attacked by a German intruder. He was buried in Leigh Cemetery, Lancashire. However, Fraser continued his visits to the Ireland's home, which possibly went some way to fill the vacuum left by Don's death.

11 Fraser's first operation in his new role took place six days after the Duisburg raid on the night of 3/4 September. The target was Brest. Initially, 140 aircraft were dispatched to attack the German battlecruisers *Scharnhorst* and *Gneisenau* undergoing repairs in the port, as well as the heavy cruiser *Prinz Eugen*, but because of worsening weather,

Headstone on Don Hodge's grave. Such was the admiration of Fraser by Mrs Ireland, that he too was added to the headstone.

most bombers were recalled. This left 53 aircraft to bomb the estimated positions of the ships through a smokescreen. No aircraft were lost but a few crash-landed on their return to England.

Fraser didn't manage to bomb Brest. "I was unable to gain sufficient height for Brest, so set course for Le Havre and when preparing to bomb, the presence of an enemy aircraft necessitated jettisoning the bombs." Fraser's flight time was 6:05 hours.

12 On the night of 7/8 September, Fraser took his crew north in a strike against the German port of Kiel, on the south Baltic coast near the Danish border. Their target was the Deutsche Werke submarine yard and surrounding area in Kiel. A total of 51 aircraft took part including three Stirlings. Good bombing was claimed in clear weather, and two passenger ships were also damaged. Flight time was 6:15 hours. On the same night 10 Stirlings were part of a 197-strong force sent to Berlin.

13 On the night of 12/13 September, Fraser returned to the target of his first operation, Frankfurt. A total of 130 aircraft took part, including nine Stirlings. Two Wellingtons were lost. Thick cloud prevented accurate bombing, but large fires were started. Frankfurt later claimed 75 high-explosive bombs and 650 incendiary bombs hit the city starting 38 fires. Mainz, nearly 20 miles away, received bombs that killed 19 people.

Of the five Stirlings on the raid from 15 Squadron, three, including Fraser's, dropped their bombs on the target area. He bombed from 15,000 feet and although many fires were observed, some were believed to be decoys. The raid took Fraser 6:20 hours.

Following this raid, Fraser spent an enjoyable five days' leave in London. He stayed in the Overseas Club, which provided cheap but excellent accommodation, and was well-patronised by New Zealanders. The city was a mecca for young airmen, with pubs and clubs, and theatres and cinemas showing the latest attractions. They could sometimes catch up with chums from other squadrons and services. For Fraser it was an opportunity to meet fellow countrymen at the New Zealand Forces' Club in Charing Cross Road or at New Zealand House. As well as

15 Squadron at Wyton, 1941. Fraser is not present in the photograph, so presumably he was on leave at the time.

participating in the social scene, Fraser visited local tourist attractions. One afternoon he and a friend took in a popular variety show, 'Apple Sauce,' featuring Max Miller, Vera Lynn and Florence Desmond. Even after five days of glitter and excitement, Fraser left London thinking, "Although I had quite a good time, I wasn't very impressed by London. It's not what it's cracked up to be except that it's very big."

14 Two weeks later, on the night of 28/29 September, Fraser flew one of the first four-engined aircraft to attack Genoa in Italy, the squadron's first operation to that country. He wrote in a letter home, "The longest trip was the last one to Italy, as we were in the air for over nine hours and I was at the controls for about seven hours." Bad weather developed, but of a more serious nature, while crossing Dunkirk on their way out, the Stirling was hit by flak which damaged the bomb release circuits, so preventing 5000 pounds of bombs in the bomb bay being released. The only bombs that could be released were those carried under the wing roots. The extent of the damage was not realised until the aircraft was on its bombing run over Genoa, and there was nothing else for it but to make the long flight back to England with the heavy bomb-load.

When they were leaving Genoa, the heavy load combined with deteriorating weather, forced Fraser to make a detour which took them

41

100 miles off course. Presumably, Fraser felt the extra weight would not allow him to achieve enough altitude in time to clear the Alps. This was serious, for it meant an unexpected drain on the remaining fuel.

The first warning of disaster came while passing the Channel Islands. The flight engineer reported that there was only enough fuel for 10 more minutes' flying. After a brief intercom conference with his crew, Fraser decided to head for England, rather than ditch into the sea or return to France where they could bail out and be taken prisoner. He chose Coastal Command's Thorney Island station on the coast near Chichester in West Sussex. Meanwhile, the flight engineer worked his magic with the remaining fuel making sure no engine was starved. At the same time, the radio operator sent out an SOS, while the remainder of the seven crew waited calmly.

Without circling Thorney Island airfield, Fraser prepared to land immediately. The four engines of the Stirling were still roaring when the giant tyres touched the concrete runway spurting blue smoke, but before the aircraft was halfway across the field, no fewer than three of the engines cut out abruptly. The Stirling was completely out of fuel and still carrying 5000 pounds of bombs. The flight had lasted 9:10 hours, Fraser's longest yet. "Not very comfortable," he remarked modestly afterwards.

39 Wellingtons and two Stirlings made the trip to Genoa, with three Wellingtons failing to return. Bomber Command claimed "successful bombing" of the target.

The next day Fraser and his crew returned their bomber to Wyton, flight time of 50 minutes, which gives an indication as to how much extra fuel is consumed to haul a 5000-pound payload.

15 The next target for Fraser was Nuremberg (Nürnberg) on the night of 15/16 October. The round trip took 7:40 hours. 80 aircraft participated – 58 Wellingtons, 13 Whitleys, five Halifaxes and four Stirlings – four Wellingtons were lost. They experienced rough conditions en route to the target, with icing and thick cloud. Only 14 aircraft claimed to have bombed Nuremberg, and 51 claimed to have bombed alternative targets. Nuremberg later claimed only three groups of bombs hit the city with one bomb destroying a Siemens factory

workshop. This was Bomber Command's second large raid on the city inside three days. The results of both raids were deemed disappointing.

As on his previous operation, Fraser ran short of fuel on his return and landed at Stradishall, Suffolk, returning to base the following day.

16 Fraser bombed Bremen on the night of 20/21 October. The flight time was 5:35 hours. It was a large attack with 153 bombers participating, including 82 Hampdens, 48 Wellingtons, 15 Stirlings and eight Manchesters (the forerunner to the Lancasters). Five aircraft were lost, but no Stirlings. Returning crews reported to have started fires in the target area, but Bremen reports described the attack as only a "small raid".

Battlecruisers kept at bay

The German battlecruisers *Scharnhorst* and *Gneisenau* arrived in Brest in April 1941, where *Prinz Eugen* joined them on 1 June after separating from *Bismarck* in the Atlantic. Because of the threat they represented to Allied shipping, their presence was of great concern to the Admiralty. Bomber Command had attacked them countless times since their arrival, but without success, although 22 Squadron of Coastal Command had disabled *Gneisenau* in a suicidal torpedo raid in early April.

Between the end of October 1941 and 10 February 1942, Fraser would complete a further five operations against Brest and the German warships, with Bomber Command hoping to destroy them, or at least incapacitate them, before they could escape back into the Atlantic to terrorise merchant shipping. All five raids would take place in darkness, Bomber Command finally realising that the losses to heavy bombers were too costly during daylight operations.

17 The first of the five further raids against Brest took place on the night of 1/2 November 1941, with only 17 aircraft taking part. Presumably these were all Stirlings, as no Stirlings took part in the major raid on Kiel on the same night. Fraser's flight time was five hours.

18 The operations on the night of 7/8 November proved to be of significance. No doubt frustrated by the recent long run of bad weather and the resulting poor bombing, Bomber Command mounted a major effort with Berlin as the main target. This decision was persisted with, despite a late weather forecast which indicated that there would be a large area of bad weather with storms, thick cloud, icing and hail over the North Sea routes that bombers would need to take to Berlin and back.

A total of 392 aircraft participated in the night's bombing, with 169 going to Berlin, 75 to Cologne and 55 to Mannheim. A further 93 aircraft were on a number of minor operations. This total probably represented the maximum number of serviceable aircraft with crews available at the time.

Fraser and his crew were in W7450, *A for Apple*, one of 17 Stirlings heading to Berlin that night – probably all from 15 and 7 Squadrons. Because of atrocious conditions encountered en route, Fraser made a calculated decision to abandon Berlin and bomb the alternative target of Münster, subsequently avoiding the mayhem experienced by other crews over Berlin. His total flight time was five hours.

Out of the 392 bombers that took part in the raid, 37 (9.4 per cent) were tragically lost. This loss was more than double the previous highest for night operations. It is possible many of the lost aircraft crashed into the North Sea on their return, after suffering icing and running out of fuel.

Not only were the British losses heavy, but the raid on Berlin could only claim fires on the outskirts of the city, with other results being largely "unobserved". Berlin later reported scattered bombing.

This operation gives an insight into the calibre of Fraser who, as an outstanding and skilled young captain, always put the safety of his crew before the sometimes audacious demands of Bomber Command.

Between 14 and 18 November Fraser took some well-earned leave. He headed up to Ambleside to be spoilt by Mrs Ireland. "It was the first time I had been up there since Don was killed in action. I met some very nice people while I was there and some of them couldn't do enough for me. One man took me out shooting one day and we got 14 rabbits." Fraser was invited to return at Christmas.

19 On the night of 23/24 November Fraser returned to Brest and the German battlecruisers. While over the target his Stirling developed a burst oil line on the port-outer engine, resulting in it being shut down. Fraser wrote home, "We went to Brest after the *Scharnhorst*. We spent over half an hour over the target and had to fight our way in through a very heavy barrage of searchlights and gunfire. For 15 minutes the searchlights held us in a cone and we could see and feel the shells bursting all round the aircraft. However, we got out again and got home safely although one engine failed." Their Stirling sustained flak damage

Stirling N3667, T for Tommy, of 15 Squadron. Wyton, 1941.

during the raid which necessitated shutting down the port-outer engine. A safe landing was made back at base. Flight time was 5:40 hours.

Only 11 bombers visited the target on that night, all of them Stirlings. Other raids on the same night were to Lorient and Dunkirk, both along the coast of France. Surprisingly, out of a total of 101 sorties, there were no losses.

After Fraser's description of the life-or-death situation above Brest, he reassured his mother of his mental toughness. "I better not tell you any more or you will be having nightmares. I did after the first two or three trips, but hardly worry at all now."

20   The attempted daytime *Circus* operation on a target along the Ruhr on 25 November proved to be Fraser's most adventurous yet. The crews of three Stirlings of 15 Squadron were given a 'roving commission' to attack any targets of opportunity. They were accompanied by a strong fighter escort hoping to lure Luftwaffe fighters into battle.

An hour out from Wyton while over the Dutch Coast, Fraser's aircraft became 'unserviceable' – the port-outer engine failed again, and they had Exactor problems. Fraser was forced to return to base, diverting in the last minutes to RAF Warboys, to the north of Wyton. Coming in to land just after midday, they crash-landed. The aircraft, Stirling 7450, *A for Apple*, which Fraser had piloted on a dozen previous occasions, was written off, but miraculously, the crew walked away from the wreckage. The other two Stirlings also aborted the operation, perhaps because of Fraser's dilemma. Fraser's flight time was 2:10 hours.

Fraser couldn't have been too shaken by the crash, as he and some mates spent the evening in London. "Three of us went up to London for the night and went to a theatre show. We stayed the night at a relation of one of the chaps."

Before the end of November, Fraser sat a night vision test assessment which he passed "above average".

During the war there were strict rules of censorship in place and describing enemy actions was forbidden. Up until now Fraser never mentioned in his letters home that he was on operations, but in a letter dated 27 November, he brought his family right up to date. Perhaps he realised after the crash that he was mortal after all. Or maybe his 20 successful operations consumed him to the extent he couldn't contain his excitement any longer. But whatever the reason for the turnaround, from then on Fraser gave at times in-depth snippets of operations, unlike many other airmen at the time.

The news must have been a bombshell for his family who probably assumed Fraser was still in training! Fraser explained that he had withheld the information in fear of it causing undue stress at home – having not forgotten that his parents originally refused him permission to go overseas.

Partway through his letter of social small talk, Fraser simply stated, "The day before yesterday I did my 20th raid on Germany" – no mention of the crash – "For ten raids I was a second pilot and the second ten I have been a captain with my own crew. I didn't say anything before as I know how you all would be worrying." Then he tried to soften the blow, "After about 30 trips we are taken off and made instructors, so by the time you get this I should be nearly finished. I've had some pretty close shaves and had a lot of luck, but I've always been sure I would come through it O.K."

Then he went on to mention the names of different places he had bombed.

21 After a couple of weeks of training flights, including an air test, circuits and landings instruction, night flying tests, a compass swinging test, a cross-country flight and a feathering airscrew test, Fraser's 21st operation was against Cologne on the night of 11/12 December, when one Halifax was lost. Only 23 of the 60 aircraft taking part reported bombing primary targets and starting a large fire, but since Cologne later

had no record of the bombs, the fire was probably a decoy. Flight time was 5:15 hours.

A couple of weeks before Christmas Fraser received a welcome parcel from home. "Your parcel with the scarf and socks [six pairs] and the [fruit] cake arrived two days ago. The cake was a real beauty and in perfect condition. It looked so good that I had a piece and now there isn't much left!" Fraser then put in his order for more goodies, all considered luxuries in war-torn Britain. "If you send any more parcels, please concentrate on tins of butter, tins of fruit etc. I should be very pleased to receive a thick polo-neck pullover from some kind person. Ailsa sent me two tins of raspberry jam which I was very pleased to get." Two pullovers were sent but were never received – Fraser wondered if they went to the bottom of the ocean. However, he did receive a pullover from a servicemen's benevolent society in Britain which he was most grateful for with winter in full swing.

22 Three nights later on 14/15 December Fraser and his crew went back to Brest. By now Bomber Command was becoming desperate to disable the battlecruisers, knowing that they were close to being seaworthy again. For Fraser it was another hectic night, with his Stirling becoming 'iced up' in 10/10 cloud experienced en route and in the target area. Not being able to gain sufficient height for bombing, he jettisoned his five 2000-pounders into the English Channel and headed home. Only 22 Hampdens and six Stirlings took part in the raid, with one Hampden being lost. One aircraft claimed to have bombed the target. Flight time was 3:45 hours.

It seems Fraser had found a regular aircraft for himself and his crew. The night's operation was his second in Stirling 3683. Fraser had already completed 11 training flights in the same aircraft, and would achieve a further two raids plus several more training flights before it disappeared from his log book.

Fraser was given leave over Christmas from 23 to 29 December, so he headed north by train to the Irelands in Westmorland. It seems Mrs Ireland had substituted Fraser for her lost son. "Mrs Ireland couldn't do enough for me and is always worrying about my catching colds and

Bombs dropping from a Stirling on German battlecruisers in Brest harbour, December 1941.

getting wet feet. On Christmas Eve we went to a great house beside one of the lakes and spent three days there. It was something like Tekapo. There were about 60 people there and although they were mostly older people, there were about a dozen of my own age.

"I spent Christmas Day tramping in a party over some of the English hills. We did about 15 miles walking over some of the most beautiful country over here." That night they had Christmas dinner and danced until midnight. On Boxing Day Fraser climbed Great Gable, the second highest peak in England (2949 feet or 899 metres), with a group of house guests. On other days he went shooting, visited local villages and went to the pictures at the local cinema.

On his last evening of leave, Mrs Ireland turned on an early 21st birthday party for Fraser – his actual birthday was 9 January.

Fraser returned by train to Wyton on 29 December. The weather had deteriorated again, hampering operations, but the men were otherwise focused on a big dance in the sergeants' mess on New Year's Eve.

23 Fraser returned to Brest for his next operation on the night of 3/4 January 1942. It was a 'minor operation' involving just four Stirlings and 14 Wellingtons, with one Wellington being lost. For

Stirling F for Freddy of 15 Squadron buzzes RAF Wyton, 1941.

Bomber Command it was a relatively quiet night, with a further 10 Hampdens minelaying in the Frisian Islands west of Denmark. Fraser's flight time was 5:25 hours.

In early January Fraser passed a medical examination for a commission, and was told that he could expect to be a pilot officer in about six weeks' time.

Fraser's 21st birthday came and went with no surprises. "I'm afraid it hasn't been any different from any other day except that I have been a bit busier than usual. It has been quite a sunny day but it has been very cold and a very chilly wind has been blowing. It wouldn't surprise me if we had snow tonight." There was snow the next morning and on many other mornings throughout January.

In a letter home at Christmas time Fraser had given a little insight to his crew. "One of the gunners in my crew [Jack Cunningham, the Irishman] was 20 last Monday and my second pilot [Jack] will be 30 tomorrow. Another of my gunners went home yesterday as his wife had a son born to her yesterday."

The second pilot, a Yorkshireman, was made a captain and left the crew after 13 operations with Fraser. His replacement was another Jack, New Zealander Flight Sergeant Jack Cowlrick, married, of Napier. Cowlrick would later be killed on 3 June 1942 when he was shot down over the Netherlands. At the time he was captaining a Stirling of 15 Squadron.

Fraser thought he had a "pretty mixed crew. There are eight of us, two New Zealanders, a Canadian, a Welshman, an Irishman (the rebel), a Londoner and two other Englishmen." Of the eight, three were married.

24   The next operation for Fraser was to Münster on the night of 22/23 January. It was the third time he had bombed the target and Bomber Command's first raid into inland Germany since 27/28 December 1941. 47 aircraft participated with one Wellington being lost. Crews reported large fires in the railway station area, but the only report from Münster records the deaths of five people with no other details. Around the time of this raid, 15 Squadron was operating from their satellite airfield at Alconbury while the runway at Wyton was being sealed. Fraser landed safely at Alconbury but their aircraft was damaged in a collision with a Wellington while taxiing. Fortunately, no one was injured. Flight time was 3:45 hours.

On 28 January Fraser flew a Stirling from Wyton to his old conversion base of Lossiemouth in Scotland. His was one of 10 Stirlings that transferred to the far north in readiness for *Operation Oiled*, a raid on the famed German battleship *Tirpitz*, deep in Trondheim Fjord, Norway. On the following day, a briefing was held for an attack that night, and eight of the Stirlings were made ready for the raid. The forecast over the target area was not encouraging, with sleet and snow and 10/10 cloud. Eventually only five of the eight took off; the others were assessed to be unserviceable and the ground crew lacked spares at the isolated station. En route, the five crews encountered worse conditions than forecasted, resulting in none of the aircraft sighting Norway. The raid was eventually called off.

With rain and snow continuing to fall at Lossiemouth, and the chance that the aircraft might get stranded if they remained at the base, further

Operation Oiled raids were abandoned.

Fraser arrived back at Wyton via Peterhead on 7 February.

25 On the night of 10/11 February, Fraser and his crew returned to Brest and the German battlecruisers for the last time. It was his sixth and final attempt at the target. Eight Stirlings and 12 Wellingtons took part with no losses. The raid was ineffectual as the target was completely covered in cloud. Six 15 Squadron Stirlings were assigned to the raid, but only four were able to get airborne. Fraser released one 2000-pound and three 500-pound bombs, but returned with four 2000-pounders still on board. He was diverted to Boscombe Downs, south of Amesbury, Wiltshire, because of bad weather at Wyton. Flight time was 4:15 hours.

The following day Fraser returned to base. On the same day, 11 February, the German Navy, in their well-executed operation code named *Operation Cerberus*, the *Scharnhorst, Gneisenau, Prinz Eugen* and a flotilla of smaller craft slipped out of Brest at 9.15pm and, escaping detection for more than 12 hours, sailed boldly into the English Channel before being discovered by a patrolling Spitfire. Despite British attacks by the RAF, the Fleet Air Arm and Coastal Artillery, by 13 February all three ships reached the safety of Germany ports after a daring dash through the Straits of Dover.

The Germans had chosen a day when bad weather and low cloud gave their ships maximum concealment. Their only setback was that the *Scharnhorst* and *Gneisenau* slowed down after striking mines laid by Bomber Command aircraft in the Frisian Islands over recent nights.

26 During 12 February, Bomber Command's response to the naval operation, later known as the Channel Dash, was tardy. Only 39 of the 242 bombers which eventually took part found and attacked the ships, but none recorded any hits. In addition to the bombers, 398 Spitfires and Hurricanes of Fighter Command flew several sorties on the same day. 35 Coastal Command Hudsons and Beauforts also took part. Altogether, 675 British aircraft took off to search for and attack the German warships.

Fraser's Stirling was one of those unsuccessful bombers on the day. All

Fraser mentioned in his log book was, "Formation search for German Navy in North Sea," indicating he was unable to locate the ships in the poor weather conditions. He flew two sorties, a two-hour daytime flight followed by a nighttime flight of similar length, landing at 20:26. Both flights combined as one operation in his personal tally.

For Bomber Command, the only positive aspect to come from the operation was that it released aircraft for other duties that would otherwise bomb ships in French ports. Bomber Command had dropped 3413 tons of bombs with limited results on the three ships in recent months and lost 127 aircraft in doing so.

Throughout the winter of 1941-42, bad weather continually hampered bombing efforts, with Fraser participating in only six operations over two months. Because he was taking longer than expected to complete his first tour of 30 operations, extra raids would be added. Fraser welcomed these, since he was enjoying operational flying so much – he had a real dread of being posted to other duties.

He explained his anxiety to his mother, "I have done 26 raids on Germany now and I heard today that I may be posted as an instructor on Stirlings in a few days. I hope not as I don't want to come off operations yet. I was supposed to go as an instructor twice lately but managed to get out of it."

By this time Fraser's parents must have become concerned about Fraser's eagerness for action, and had resorted to cabling Fraser occasionally to check on his wellbeing. Fraser's reaction to this was, "… and please don't cable to see if I'm O.K." Eventually, Fraser's first tour would run out to 39 operations.

However, Fraser didn't have it all his way. During February he undertook some instructor's duties on Stirlings while still on operational duties with 15 Squadron. For four nights he took training pilots for "night landings instruction" as well as cross-country flights during daytime.

Bomber's moon

Air Chief Marshal Sir Arthur Harris, nicknamed "Bomber Harris", took charge of Bomber Command on 22 February 1942. With him came the famous 'area bombing' directive from the Air Ministry: "It has been decided that the primary objective of your operations should now be focused on the morale of the enemy civil population and in particular the industrial workers." It was clear the 'aiming points' were to be built-up areas and not dockyards, aircraft factories or other industrial targets.

Harris inherited a force of aircraft no stronger in numbers than a year before. The continuing drain of squadrons to Coastal Command and the Middle East and the heavy operational losses of 1941 had prevented any build-up in total strength. Numbers at 1 March 1942 showed a total strength of 469 night bombers and 78 day bombers. But the calibre of the force had improved, with bigger and more powerful aircraft coming on stream and increased bomb-carrying capacity.

Alongside the increase in bomb tonnage came the first major improvement in navigation. This was *Gee*, a device that enabled a bomber's navigator to fix his position by operating an instrument – the *Gee* Box – which received pulse signals from three widely separated transmitting stations in England. *Gee* computed the difference between the three signals and gave the navigator an instant 'fix'. As it was a line-of-sight device, the curvature of the earth limited its range – an aircraft flying at 20,000 feet 400 miles from England could just receive the signals. For targets outside this range, *Gee* could still be used in getting aircraft started in the right direction.

The major benefit of *Gee* was it enabled crews to reach the general area of a target, preventing them going badly off course in strong winds and overcast conditions. *Gee* also helped crews to find their way home.

Harris immediately introduced some tactical improvements. These included the principle of concentrating bombs on a single target. So rather than bomb two or three targets on the same night with the

Bombing up Stirling N6101. Bomber aircraft were usually spread out in dispersal areas to contain damage if there was an accidental bomb detonation.

bombing spread over several hours, Bomber Command would attack one main target with bombing concentrated in a period of just two hours or less. Harris also believed that it was easier to burn a city down than to blow it up, so sanctioned the widespread use of incendiaries.

So the macabre recipe for a city's destruction was: open the raid with ordinary high-explosive bombs to crater and block roads with fallen masonry to prevent fire engines moving around the city; followed with blast bombs and incendiaries. The blast bombs blew off roofs and smashed windows and the incendiaries penetrated the roofs and started fires which were fed by air drawn in through the broken windows.

The best results were attained by moonlight. During the early years of the war the expression "bomber's moon" replaced "full moon" – bombers

15 Squadron Stirlings flying over English countryside.

used the moonlight to visually locate their targets. But later in the war, this strategy would mostly change as navigational aids improved and the threat of German night fighters increased.

With these 'improvements' it was now clear to the Air Ministry that air superiority would be the decisive factor in the battle against Germany. The bomber crews now had the tasteless job of dropping their payloads on civilians.

Fraser took some leave from 25 February to 3 March to stay with friends in Kent. This was his first break since Christmas. "I had a very nice time. It was quiet, but I enjoyed it and had a good rest. They gave me breakfast in bed every morning so it suited me down to the ground."

In early March Fraser heard again that he might be posted as an instructor on Stirlings. He still hoped to remain on operations. Perhaps it had something to do with crew loyalty. Because Fraser flew with Boggis and Ogilvie for his first 10 operations, his own crew had flown fewer missions. He may have wanted them all to complete their first tour together – a typical Fraser Barron gesture.

27 The next action for Fraser came in early March when he attacked Essen on the night of 8/9 March. It was the first of three raids on the city in just 48 hours. Harris attempted to bring new strategies into play with Essen being the only major target on the night. 211 aircraft took part, including 27 Stirlings. For Harris it was yet another step forward – a heavy raid on the previously difficult target, with the leading bombers fitted with *Gee*. Although it was a fine night, industrial haze over Essen prevented accurate bombing.

The raid was considered a disappointment. Photographic evidence taken the next morning showed that the main targets within the city, the Krupps factories, were not hit but some bombs fell in the southern part of Essen. Eight aircraft were lost including one Stirling. Fraser's flight time was 4:15 hours.

28 The following night, 9/10 March, Essen was again the main target. This time 187 aircraft joined the raid with three aircraft being lost. Again, thick ground haze led to scattered bombing. Only two buildings in Essen were destroyed and 72 damaged. Incredibly, bombs fell on 24 other Ruhr towns.

Fraser didn't even make it to the target. During the climb out over the North Sea, the front turret door flew open and, because of damage to the hinges, it could not be closed. Rather than risk the door breaking free and smashing into a propeller, he abandoned the operation. Unlike non-claims on some later abandoned raids, the operation was still added to Fraser's tally. His total flight time was 2:45 hours.

29 The final raid in the trilogy happened the next night, 10/11 March, with 126 aircraft bombing Essen, again the main target for the night. Four aircraft, including one Stirling, were lost. This raid was significant because it was the first major night-operation for the new four-engined Lancaster – two of them took part. Their first appearance had occurred a week earlier when four Lancasters laid mines off the German coast.

This was another disappointing raid with unexpected cloud being the main cause for poor bombing. 62 crews, half the force, claimed to have bombed Essen, and 35 crews bombed alternative targets. Contrary to these claims, Essen later reported that two bombs fell on railway lines near the Krupps factory, one house was destroyed and two damaged in residential areas. Five Germans were killed and a Polish worker was killed by a flak shell which descended and exploded on the ground.

Fraser's aircraft was among the 35 that claimed to have bombed alternative targets. He believed he had bombed Gelsenkirchen. Because of deteriorating weather at Wyton on Fraser's return, he was diverted to Marham, northeast of Cambridge.

All three raids on Essen were ineffectual. Harris was hoping that *Gee* would help to produce devastating bombing results on this important but usually haze-concealed target, but for the little damage achieved, Britain lost 15 crews – about 84 men – over the three nights.

All Fraser could say about the raids was, "I went on three raids to Germany. We did them on three successive nights and I was pretty tired at the end of it. We went to Essen on the Ruhr and had a pretty good time although it was a bit hot at times. I have now done 29 raids and will be finished soon." It seems Fraser was for the first time looking forward to his break from bombing.

During mid March Fraser did a daylight air-to-sea firing exercise with the turret guns while flying low over the Wash estuary, north of East Anglia. This implied to both Fraser and his crew that a nautical operation was imminent.

30 Fraser had a different assignment for his next operation – he was ordered to lay mines off Lorient on the night of 23/24 March. Lorient was selected because of its proximity to an important U-boat base. Fraser's aircraft was one of three Stirlings present out of a total of 17 aircraft. None was lost. It was the only Bomber Command operation on the night and the first time Stirlings or four-engined aircraft were used for minelaying, known amongst bomber crews as 'gardening'. After 6:20 hours flying Fraser touched down at Boscombe Downs and returned to base later the next day.

But the operation was not without problems. While making a run prior to releasing its mines, Fraser's Stirling was hit by light flak. A single shell penetrated the fuselage behind the door and exploded, cutting the

Loading 1500-pound mines into the narrow Stirling bomb bay proved a difficult task for ground crew.

trimming wires and throwing such a heavy weight on the controls that Fraser was unable to hold them steady by himself. Jack Cowlrick helped and between them they managed to fly the Stirling to Boscombe Downs. After landing they found 29 holes caused by the exploding shell.

All Fraser revealed in a letter home was, "Three nights ago we went minelaying in enemy waters and had quite an exciting time." He was also excited about being commissioned as a Pilot Officer on 23 March.

31 Fraser returned to Essen on the night of 25/26 March. The major raid involved 254 aircraft, including 26 Stirlings and seven Lancasters. It was the largest raid of the war so far with nine aircraft being lost. Visibility was good and over 180 crews claimed to have bombed Essen, and many claiming to have hit the Krupps works. But bombing photographs showed that much of the effort was drawn to a large decoy fire at Rheinberg, 18 miles west of Essen. Essen later reported that only nine high-explosive bombs hit the city. The raid was another disappointment for Harris, since the target still eluded him. Fraser's flight time was exactly four hours.

The nerve centre of a Stirling bomber.

32 Three nights later on 28/29 March, Fraser raided Lübeck, a port southeast of Kiel, with a payload of incendiaries. For Bomber Command it was a major raid by 234 aircraft, including 26 Stirlings. 12 aircraft were lost, including three Stirlings – the most yet on a single operation.

This raid was the first major success against a German target by Bomber Command. The attack was carried out in good visibility with the help of an almost full moon. Because of the light defences over the target, bomber crews descended to low altitudes, some as low as 2000 feet. The Main Force attacked in three waves, with experienced crews flying *Gee*-fitted aircraft in the first wave.

Fraser and his crew were in the first wave. He was carrying a number of the new 250-pound incendiary bombs. Bombing from 16,000 feet his incendiaries were observed to fall "clean across the town." So intense were the flames, that Fraser's crew could still observe them from 80 miles away on their return. His flight time was 5:30 hours.

Over two thirds of the 400 tons of bombs dropped that night were incendiary. 191 crews claimed successful attacks. From reconnaissance photographs it was established that approximately 190 acres of the central city were destroyed, mostly by fire. Over 300 people were killed on the ground, the heaviest death toll in a raid on a German target so far in the war.

Lübeck was not bombed again during the war, as the port was later used for the shipment of Red Cross supplies, including those distributed to Allied prisoners of war.

About this time, larger gaps started to appear between Fraser's letters home, making it more difficult to maintain a continuity of events. It is presumed that many letters were lost in transit or have gone missing from family records. In the letters that have survived, Fraser still maintained his easy style of writing, giving a good commentary of an airman's life in war-torn Britain.

33 Fraser's next raid was the bombing of the Poissy Ford motor plant, located 21 miles outside Paris in the small town of Poissy, on the night of 2/3 April. Bomber Command aimed to minimise the deaths of French civilians living near the plant using low-level precision bombing. On the previous night, 41 aircraft bombed the plant, but a photographic flight that morning showed the raid was unsuccessful. Bomber Command decided to revisit the target with 40 Wellingtons and 10 Stirlings, of which one Wellington was lost. This second operation was considered successful. Fraser's flight took 4:40 hours.

34 Fraser returned to Cologne a few nights later on the night of 5/6 April. 263 aircraft took part in the raid. Five aircraft were lost but all 29 Stirlings returned safely. This raid was a new record for a force being sent to a single target, in this case the Humboldt works in the Deutz area of Cologne. 211 crews claimed success, but photographic

evidence told the familiar story of scattered bombing – the nearest bombs falling some five miles from the target. Fraser's flight time was 5:30 hours.

35 Only three nights later, on 8/9 April, Fraser raided Hamburg for the first time. 272 aircraft took part, including 22 Stirlings. Five aircraft were lost. This raid set yet another record for aircraft bombing a single target.

Icing and electrical storms were encountered over Germany. Although 188 aircraft reported bombing within the target area, the operation was a failure as the equivalent of only 14 aircraft bomb-loads fell on the city. Nearby Bremen later reported a bomb-load of incendiaries was dropped on a shipyard within the city. Fraser's flight took six hours.

After this operation Fraser took a week's leave enjoying the warmer days of spring with the Irelands at Ambleside. He wrote, "a wonderful time" with the weather "like the middle of summer." Before travelling to Ambleside, Fraser spent two days in London ordering new uniforms, now that he was commissioned. In all, they cost £65 of which the RAF paid £45. The cost was not a problem to Fraser, as his minimal-drinking habits allowed him to save. He was often a 'banker' to his mates whenever they fell short.

On his eventual return to Wyton, Fraser switched quarters to the officers' mess, acquiring the services of a batman. "I've got a really good batman who does everything. He wakes me up in the morning at a quarter to eight and brings me a cup of tea in bed. He cleans my buttons and shoes, and makes the bed. In fact, it's almost like home with you and the aunts spoiling me!"

36 Fraser returned to 'gardening' on the night of 22/23 April, in an exhaustive flight of 7:10 hours to minelay in Kiel Bay on the Baltic. On the night, 63 aircraft were minelaying off Germany and Denmark. Of these, one Hampden was lost.

37 Fraser had no time to recover from this operation, as he completed an equally-arduous operation the very next night on 23/24 April. The target was Rostock, further east from Kiel. 161 aircraft took part, including 31 Stirlings – the most on any raid that Fraser took

A bomber crew walks past Stirling N3676, S for Sugar, while a member of the ground crew runs up the engines. Fraser piloted this aircraft on 16 July 1942 while with 1651 HCU, Waterbeach, completing a dual circuit and landing instruction flight with Pilot Officer Quinn as second pilot.

part in. Four aircraft were lost. Fraser's flight time was seven hours.

On the same raid some bombers from 5 Group attempted to precision-bomb the Heinkel aircraft factory to the south of the city.

This was the first of a series of four raids on the Baltic port. Each raid was similar to the recent bombing of Lübeck, with the use of incendiaries in a concentrated area and only light defences. But the results of the first raid were disappointing as only scattered bombing was reported.

38 Just two nights later on 25/26 April, Fraser and his crew were returning to Rostock, but an hour and a half out from England their port-outer engine had to be shut down, forcing them to abandon the operation. The flight of 3:35 hours counted towards Fraser's final tally.

After the four raids on Rostock, Bomber Command finally got their bomb mix to a lethal ratio – one third high explosive and two thirds incendiary. For subsequent bombing this would be the norm. The Germans acknowledged the raids by naming the new bomb mix "Terrorangriff," meaning terrorist raid.

39 The raid on the night of 27/28 April was Fraser's last to complete his first tour. The target was Cologne with 97 aircraft taking part – 19 of them Stirlings. Seven aircraft were lost. Good results were claimed but a considerable number of bombs fell outside the city to the east. On the same night 43 Halifaxes and Lancasters attacked the *Tirpitz* in Trondheim Fjord, Norway.

That night Fraser's crew comprised Pilot Officers Kennedy and Hack, and Sergeants Bebbington, Long, Meades, Jackson and Cunningham. Their bomb-load was four 2000-pounders.

'Rest' from operations

At last Fraser had finished his first tour. His next appointment would be as an instructor with 1651 HCU at Waterbeach, five miles north of Cambridge, not far from Wyton.

A first operational tour on heavy bombers usually consisted of 30 operations, but Fraser's tally somewhat overran this mark to 39 operations. In his log book he pencilled the total operational flying hours for the 39 raids as 200:10 hours.

After a tour, aircrew were rested for about six months, usually instructing at training or conversion units. That 'rest' was, however, in name only, as more than 8000 men were killed in non-operational flying accidents in Britain. After the rest period, they were obligated to do a second operational tour of a further 20 operations.

Fraser was one of the lucky ones to complete his first tour. The average number of completed operations for a Bomber Command airman was about 14. For the war so far the aircraft loss-rate per operation hovered around 5%, or about one in 20 aircraft being lost. Some operations were much higher.

Bomber Command would finally lose 55,500 aircrew (44%) out of a total of 125,000 aircrew on active service. The losses were made up of 47,300 aircrew killed or 'missing' while in action against the enemy, and 8200 dying in non-operational activities such as training in Britain. Approximately 6000 New Zealanders served with Bomber Command, and of those 1850 lost their lives.

The average age of all those killed was about 25 years. Any crewman in his early thirties was considered 'old' by his comrades. Yet they bore a mature responsibility upon their shoulders.

None of them believed fighting the Germans would be a picnic. It was tough all right. Crewmen wondered how their families would react if they knew just how merciless it was, knowing that they might never come back. Only a few back home knew to what extent luck decided

Fraser with Mrs Ireland, Ambleside, 1941.

their fate.

Death was always lurking. Although airmen talked about the merits of a quick death, without prior knowledge or pain, none wanted – or expected – to die.

Dying was always for the other blokes whose luck had run out. Every airman wanted a life with a future that stretched far beyond the next operation – a life with no more killing and no more being shot at.

Fraser's crew considered him a good captain. Good captains made quick and competent decisions, mostly derived from experience. Remaining a few extra seconds over a hot target often determined survival or death. One second their bomber might be roaring across the sky, and the next it could be torn apart by a German shell.

Fraser, a bomber captain at just 21 years, coolly, cheerfully, and skilfully led his crew, night after night, knowing too well that their chances of survival were slim.

There seemed to be a trend for successful pilots to be decorated after the completion of a tour. For Fraser the pattern was no different, for he was immediately recommended for the DFM, even though he had been commissioned on 23 March 1942, making him eligible for the officers' award, the DFC. In a letter home he wrote, "If I get it don't be surprised. On the other hand, don't be surprised if I don't get it. It will take another six weeks to come through, if it comes at all."

In early May Fraser was given a good chunk of leave before he was required to report to Waterbeach. First he travelled to Scotland on 5 May to stay with Mr and Mrs Caie in Aberdeen, who did everything they could to make his stay a happy one. "Yesterday we took a bus and went up the River Dee to a place called Banchory about 20 miles from Aberdeen and spent the afternoon there." In the evening they took in a show starring a local comedian. "Some of it was lost on me because it was all spoken in broad Scottish."

"Me-onie," the home of Mr and Mrs Ireland, Ambleside, beside Lake Windermere, Lake District.

After leaving Aberdeen, Fraser travelled alone for a week or so, taking in some attractions of Scotland, before a stay with the Irelands at Ambleside. For Fraser, staying with the Caies and Irelands certainly went some way to compensate for the family

Mr and Mrs Ireland on the front porch of Me-onie.

life he missed in New Zealand. He then travelled south, visiting London before stopping at Wyton to prepare for his shift to Waterbeach.

On 21 May Fraser arrived in style at Waterbeach – he flew in from Wyton aboard a Stirling, acting as second pilot to Pilot Officer De Ville.

One of the first things Fraser noticed was that Waterbeach was situated on the flight path for many squadrons heading to Europe. "We are quite close to the coast here and there have been a lot of squadrons of fighters going overhead on their way to France."

After being rested from operations and taking some leave, Fraser was more relaxed knowing that his "fighting days were over for a while." It seems Fraser had settled well into his new role. "I don't do very much flying and get seven days' leave every seven weeks and odd days off if we want it, so that will suit me down to the ground. I went for a walk today in the wood. As it's spring here all the wild flowers are out and the wood was covered with primroses, violets and bluebells."

Completely taken by surprise, Fraser was ordered back to Wyton after only a week of being an instructor in his new unit. In that time he managed five instructor daytime flights. Fraser later explained, "I was posted at once to a training station not very far from my old station. However, I had only been an instructor for a week when I was sent back to the old squadron to take part in the big 1000-aircraft attack on Cologne."

While he was still at Waterbeach, Fraser's DFM came through on 26 May. The Official Citation reads: "Flight Sergeant Barron has completed 29 operational flights as captain of the aircraft. These sorties include attacks on targets at Berlin, Frankfurt, Bremen and Brest. He has proved himself to be most reliable, efficient and courageous, pressing home his attacks regardless of opposition. His keenness and enthusiasm have set a very high example to his crew and squadron." The recommendation for Fraser's DFM was made on completion of his tour of 39 operations, 29 of those as captain of the aircraft and the rest as second pilot.

Fraser was modest. "I got the DFM about a week ago but I suppose you know about that by now," was all he wrote about the award at the time. At the end of July he wrote of the unfairness of his award. "I am glad you are pleased about the DFM as it will probably mean more to you and Dad than it does to me. I'm afraid it doesn't mean much to me. There were eight of us in my crew, all doing the same job and taking the same risks. I don't think it is right or fair that one of us, myself least of all, should have been picked out and decorated. There were also dozens of fellas whom I knew well and who were shot down before they had a chance to be recommended for decorations."

The following day Pilot Officer James Fraser Barron DFM left Waterbeach the same way he arrived – he flew a Stirling back to Wyton.

A thousand bombers

Bomber Harris was determined to capitalise on the recent area-bombing successes at Lübeck and Rostock. He knew that the future existence of Bomber Command was still in doubt, so he approached both the Prime Minister Winston Churchill and Air Chief Marshal Sir Charles Portal, Chief of the Air Staff, with the suggestion of a massive 1000-bomber raid on a German city. Both were impressed by the idea.

The 1000-bomber raids could prove useful propaganda for the Allies – particularly for Harris – and the concept of a strategic bombing offensive. Bomber Command's poor performance in bombing accuracy during 1941 had led to calls for the force to be split up and diverted to other theatres, such as the Battle of the Atlantic.

A headline-grabbing heavy raid on Germany could be a way to demonstrate to the War Cabinet that, given the investment in numbers and technology, Bomber Command could make a vital contribution to final victory.

Harris also hoped the devastation from such massive raids might be enough to knock Germany out of the war, or at least severely damage German industry and morale.

Harris only had a little over 400 front-line bombers on hand, but he did have a considerable number of additional aircraft in conversion units. These second-line bombers could be crewed by a combination of instructors, many of them ex-operational like Fraser, and by men in the later stages of training. Harris also asked for help from Coastal Command, who declined to participate, and Flying Training Command, who accepted.

Fraser was ordered to return briefly to active service, quickly going back to 15 Squadron to team up with his regular crew. He was excited at being involved in something big – already he had found instructing to be tedious.

Final orders for the raid were ready on 26 May 1942, coinciding with

Stirling A for Apple of 15 Squadron. Wyton 1941.

the approaching full moon. The massive force stood ready, waiting for suitable weather conditions. Harris decided on Cologne, the third largest city in Germany, as the target.

40 Meanwhile, "I did a minelaying trip in enemy waters to get my hand in again." Fraser volunteered for the 'gardening' operation on the night of 29/30 May, knowing that the 'big raid' was imminent with the full moon now upon them. The operation took them to the Frisian Islands off Copenhagen, with 21 aircraft participating. Fraser's flight time was 5:35 hours.

41 Soon after noon on 30 May the order to attack Cologne went out to the groups and squadrons for the 'big raid' to take place that night. The previous major raid was to Mannheim on 19/20 May, so the Germans must have been apprehensive after 10 days of just minor operations.

Code named *Operation Millennium*, the first 1000-bomber raid had 1047 aircraft flying on the night, made up of 602 Wellingtons, 131 Halifaxes, 88 Stirlings, 79 Hampdens, 73 Lancasters, 46 Manchesters and 28 Whitleys. The number of aircraft that claimed to have bombed on the night was slightly less than 900, with the extra aircraft mostly out for a 'joyride'. The total weight of bombs dropped was 1455 tons, two thirds of which were incendiaries.

German records later showed that 2500 fires were started. But there was no 'sea of fire' as Cologne was a modern city with wide streets. An estimated 12,840 buildings were either destroyed or damaged. About

480 people were killed and 45,000 made homeless.

The success of the operation came at a high price; 41 aircraft were lost – the highest number on any raid yet.

Afterwards, Fraser wrote home, "The Cologne raid was a great trip and I had a fairly easy time. It was such a clear moonlit night that we were able to bomb the very centre of the city." In his log book he made a rare comment, "Raid on Cologne. Over 1000 bombers were used for the first time on this raid." Fraser's flight time was 4.55 hours.

Fraser pictured at Ambleside wearing his newly-awarded DFM ribbon below his wings.

42 Just two nights later on 1/2 June, the 1000-bomber raid was repeated on Essen, although only 956 aircraft could be mustered on the night. Included in this total were 77 Stirlings. The plan was similar to the previous raid, except that more flares were dropped by the 'raid leaders' flying Wellingtons from 3 Group.

The results were extremely disappointing for Bomber Command, as haze or a layer of low cloud hampered accurate bombing. Essen later reported just 11 houses destroyed and 184 damaged, mostly to the south of the city. Again the cost was high with 31 bombers lost. Fraser's flight time was 3:45 hours.

Regardless of the results, Churchill seemed highly impressed and sanctioned further raids on the same scale, but not until the next favourable moon later in the month.

Now that 1000-bomber raids were to be forgotten about for the time

A Stirling of 1651 HCU being bombed up for a 1000-bomber raid. The Stirling's bomb bay is split into three narrow compartments making it unsuitable for larger bombs such as the 4000-pounder. 250-pound bombs are being placed in racks in the wing roots.

being, Fraser flew back to Waterbeach the following day, a flight of only 15 minutes. He had flown three out of the last four nights and was exhausted. That night he ended a short letter with, "I'm afraid I'll have to stop now as I'm very tired, but I'll have plenty of opportunity to make up for lost sleep on this station."

During the following week, Fraser was allowed to rest up before commencing his instructor duties. "The Duke of Kent paid a visit to our station about three days ago and the King and Queen came today [11 June]." On 14 June, Fraser was back on instructor's duties when he took Pilot Officer Baigent and his crew cross-country to the Isle of Man and back, a flight of over five hours. Other duties over the following days were mostly air tests, circuits and landings and night flight tests.

43 With the return of the full moon, another 1000-bomber raid was planned for the night of 25/26 June, this time to Bremen. Although only 960 aircraft took part, every type of aircraft flown by Bomber Command was included, even Bostons and Mosquitoes of 2 Group, which so far had only been used for day operations. Fraser's

Stirling was one of 69 on the night. The tactics were similar to the previous 1000-bomber raids, except that the bombing period was now reduced to 65 minutes.

During the day, cloud covered Bremen, but Bomber Command hoped this would be pushed to the east by strong winds. Unfortunately the wind dropped in the evening and the force encountered 10/10 cloud over the target. The limited success of the raid was due entirely to the lead bombers using *Gee* which enabled them to start fires. This allowed following aircraft to bomb the glow through the clouds. The Germans claimed 52 aircraft shot down, but the actual figure was 48, a new record, nonetheless.

For the raid, Fraser flew a Stirling directly from 1651 HCU at Waterbeach, rather than return to Wyton. He later reported, "10/10 cloud at target. Bombed Wilhelmshaven" on the North Sea instead, taking five hours' flying time. In a letter home, Fraser briefly described the raid as, "a pretty good and interesting trip."

Fraser and his crew alongside Stirling N6044. (l-r): "Larry, rear gunner; Fraser, skipper; Shep, 2nd pilot; Jacko, engineer; Bill, wireless operator; Vie, navigator. Absent: Jack, mid gunner; Sam, front gunner." Larry is holding up his lucky rabbit's foot, which he claimed brought them home from each raid.

At the end of June, Fraser travelled to Portsmouth to be stationed with an anti-aircraft battery for three days, providing him with an opportunity to exchange ideas, having been on the receiving end of flak for some months.

Fraser was kept busy instructing at Waterbeach for most of July, flying the majority of flights in daytime. Training flights took him to Stradishall, West Freugh, Wyton, Oakington and Halton air bases. The most common flying instruction was dual circuits and landings. Fraser commented, "I have been pretty busy this last month and have trained three pilots to fly Stirlings both in daytime and at night. I have now started on a fourth, a New Zealander." The Kiwi was Flight Lieutenant Frank Gatland DFM of Onehunga, who spent the last two years of the war as a prisoner of war after being shot down.

On the night of 23/24 July, while Fraser was training a pilot officer named Thornton, "the Germans came over and started to bomb several towns nearby. All the aerodrome lights, including the flare path, were put out and we were stuck up in the air for two hours." However, Fraser and his crew had an interesting time viewing the raid and "had the pleasure of seeing several Jerries shot down."

By now the tedium was getting to Fraser who wrote home, "I've been an instructor now for about two months and am getting a bit fed up with it." In the same letter Fraser included a photograph of his first tour's regular crew. There are only six crewmen pictured; a further two were absent [see photograph on previous page]. Fraser mentioned, "We did over 20 raids together. The chap on the end is Larry the rear gunner, and he is holding up his lucky rabbit's foot which he swears was the only thing which brought us back every time."

44 Fraser's next raid was on the cold summer's night of 28/29 July when he flew again from Waterbeach. The operation was a major raid on Hamburg, the second against the target in just three nights. The bomber force comprised 256 aircraft, of which 71 were Stirlings – including 12 from Waterbeach. Fraser's aircraft 9304, *U for Uncle*, suffered severe icing, forcing him to abandon the operation near Hamburg. His was one of 34 aircraft that turned back. The Stirling lacked de-icing equipment and did not have the power to climb above

F for Freddie of 15 Squadron coming in to land.

the bad weather. Most crews experienced icing, with only 68 aircraft claiming to have bombed in the target area. Losses were heavy – 30 aircraft did not return from the raid which produced poor results.

Fraser later wrote home, "We were in the air for five hours and didn't see the ground from the time we took off until we got back, as we were in cloud all the time. We were very disappointed at having to turn back as we had nearly reached the target but our aircraft was icing up so badly that all our windows were iced over and one chunk of ice broke our astrodome. It was the worst night I have ever been out in."

Fraser's crew on the night was Pilot Officers Thornton and Frazer, and Sergeants Clegg, Allen, Ward, Anslow and Gray.

Everyone was sad at Waterbeach the following day, as four of their 12 aircraft assigned to the previous night's operation failed to return; 31 young men were reported as missing in action. Of the 12 aircraft, three failed to take off, four returned after severe icing, one returned with mechanical problems and four were lost.

Fraser wrote, "Out of nine of us from our station, only five of us got back to England. The others," Fraser said hopefully, "must have been forced down on the other side." This last comment was probably aimed at his mother, in the hope of diminishing the catastrophic outcome of the raid.

Fraser stands outside his barracks. The DFM ribbon can be seen below his wings.

45 Three nights later on 31 July / 1 August, Fraser and his Waterbeach crew bombed Düsseldorf in another mass raid on a German city. 630 aircraft took part including 61 Stirlings. It was the first raid of the war when more than 100 Lancasters took part. Crews of 484 aircraft later claimed successful bombing, although their photographs showed that part of the force had bombed open country! The casualties were again high with 29 bombers being lost. Fraser's flight time was 4:20 hours. In his log book he pencilled a running total of 228:55 hours on operations to date.

After the Düsseldorf raid Fraser settled down to the drudgery of instructor's duties. There were the usual cross-country flights, night landings, circuits and landings, and air tests. His log book states that during August he trained seven different pilots to fly Stirlings. One of these was Pilot Officer Jack Paape, a former student and house master at Waitaki Boys' High, Fraser's old school. But Fraser did manage some leave in early August to visit the Irelands at Ambleside.

46 Fraser's next operation was a return trip to Düsseldorf on the night of 10/11 September. His second pilot was his pupil, Pilot Officer Jack Paape. Training and conversion aircraft were again a major part of the 479-strong force of which 33 aircraft were lost. Pathfinders successfully marked the target using TIs (target indicators) in converted 4000-pound bomb casings, dubbed 'Pink Pansies,' for the first time. Although defences at Düsseldorf had recently been strengthened, the raid was one of Bomber Command's more successful of 1942. This was Fraser's first raid where the newly-formed Pathfinder Force took part.

The Düsseldorf raid was Fraser's last operation while based at Waterbeach with 1651 HCU. It is interesting to note that after Fraser completed his tour of 39 operations, Bomber Command almost immediately decided to employ OTU and Conversion Unit (CU) instructors, crews and aircraft on major operations, starting with the 1000-bomber raids. So, at a time when Fraser was meant to be resting from operational service, he still completed seven front-line operations while stationed at Waterbeach.

At the end of his 'rest' tour, Fraser volunteered to be posted to an operational Bomber Command squadron for the usual second tour requirement of 20 operations. But first he took a week's leave at Ambleside in mid September.

On 20 September, on his return from leave, Fraser was posted to 7 Squadron based at Oakington, northwest of Cambridge, between his former RAF stations of Waterbeach and Wyton. Fraser's war to date had been confined to one small corner of Cambridgeshire.

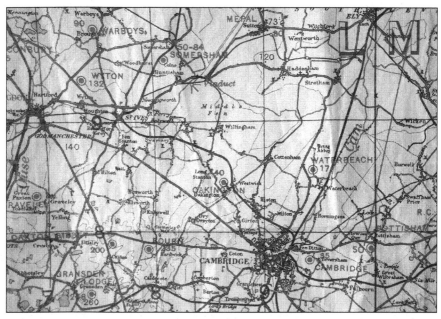

Portion of an official RAF navigation map. Three of Fraser's stations are caught in one small corner of Cambridgeshire – to the left is Wyton, to the right is Waterbeach, and between them is Oakington.

On tour again

Fraser's new unit was a founding squadron of the Pathfinder Force which had recently been established on 15 August 1942 with headquarters at Fraser's old base of Wyton. The nucleus of the Pathfinder Force, which constituted the new 8th Bomber Command Group, was five squadrons  – one taken from each of the operational Bomber Command groups. 7 Squadron, flying Stirlings, was taken from 3 Group. All five squadrons were stationed on adjacent airfields within 3 Group's sector and near to Cambridge. This elite group was commanded by Group Captain Don Bennett, an Australian. The function of the new force was to locate and mark targets with flares, which a following bomber force could aim at to increase the accuracy of their bombing.

On his very first day at Oakington, Fraser and most of his newly-formed crew did an air test, which was more of a familiarisation flight for

Bombing up Stirling G for George, 7 Squadron, Oakington.

Fraser with the crew of his second tour in front of Stirling R9255, G for George, piloted by Fraser on raids 59-61 during February 1943. (l-r): JE Robbins, J Marshall, W Mayson, Fraser, PE Turner, JW Roch, PR Coldwell.

the crew. Fraser personally selected his new crew, looking for combat experience and ability. The crew was: Flight Sergeant PR Coldwell, navigator; Flight Sergeant JW Roch, wireless operator; Sergeant HA Wade, flight engineer; Sergeant W Mayson, front gunner; Pilot Officer JR (Jack) Cunningham, rear gunner; and Pilot Officer J Marshall, mid-upper gunner. On 24 September Fraser flew a Stirling to RAF Chipping Warden to personally collect Jack Cunningham, and bring him back to Oakington. Four of the crew would remain with Fraser for the duration of his second tour.

Fraser belonged to A Flight which was commanded by the legendary Squadron Leader Hamish Mahaddie. Over the following days the crew honed their skills while completing cross-country flights and air tests. By the beginning of October they were ready for action.

47 They didn't have long to wait as their first operation together was on the night of 2/3 October against Krefeld, an important engineering centre on the west bank of the lower Rhine, not far from Holland. Out of a bombing force of 188 aircraft participating, 23 were Stirlings. The 18 Pathfinder aircraft encountered dense haze and their

marking was late. Four aircraft of this group were to release long sticks of reconnaissance flares across the target area to assist identification, while the other 14 were to drop short flare sticks, plus 250-pound incendiaries. The resulting raid was dispersed and not expected to cause much damage. 10 aircraft were lost.

Fraser must have been inspired by reading other log books between tours, as he began to give a brief summary of each raid. Of Krefeld he wrote, "Load: 3 x 2000, 2 x 1000. Two runs over target. Large concentrations of S/Ls [searchlights]. Moderate heavy flak. Accurate. Four photos. Height 14,000 feet. Descended to 1000 feet over Holland on return. Caught near coast by S/Ls and light flak." As they were newcomers to the Pathfinders on this raid, Fraser and his crew carried only a load of high explosive bombs. The flight took four hours.

48 Four nights later on 6/7 October, Fraser and his crew returned to Germany to bomb Osnabrück, an important industrial town and railway junction. The bombing force was 237 strong and six aircraft were lost. This time Fraser carried "25 x 3 flares". The Pathfinders succeeded in illuminating the Dümmer See, a large lake northeast of the

Fraser with the crew of his second tour backed by their ground crew, 7 Squadron, Oakington, February 1943. Behind them is a Stirling. (l-r): JE Robbins, J Marshall, W Mayson, PE Turner, PR Coldwell, Fraser, JW Roch.

A close up of a Stirling bomber over England.

target that was cleverly used as a run-in point. Fraser wrote, "Intense S/ Ls. Little flak. One photo obtained."

The bombing of Osnabrück was well concentrated, with most of the attack falling in the centre and the southern part of the city. The encouraging results were a major boost to the Pathfinders. During his bombing run at 14,000 feet, Fraser's aircraft was attacked by a Ju88 night fighter. Fraser immediately dived to 10,000 feet to evade the enemy. This was Fraser's first attack by a night fighter. Just five minutes later they were attacked by a second Ju88, which Fraser also managed to shake off.

In his usual matter-of-fact fashion to his mother, "We had a bit of excitement on the second trip when two night fighters attacked us over the target within five minutes of each other. However, we managed to beat them off." Fraser's Stirling could quite easily have become the seventh aircraft lost on the night. His flight time was 4:45 hours.

Fraser was promoted to Flight Lieutenant on 6 October, skipping the in-between rank of Flying Officer. "I guess I must be pretty lucky as I was a sergeant only six months ago. My pay goes up about five bob a day." In mid October, Fraser spent a week's leave with the Irelands at Ambleside. "The weather has not been very good. It has been misty all the time and a lot of fog hanging around the tops of the hills."

Targeting the soft underbelly

Late in October 1942, Bomber Command shifted considerable focus to industrial targets in northern Italy. Their aim was to smash the industries contributing to operations in North Africa, and possibly help to knock Italy out of the war. Churchill often referred to Italy and Sicily as the soft underbelly of the Axis. At first only three cities, Milan, Turin and Genoa, were considered targets, as bombers could reach them from Britain, and return to their home bases. The first strike in the new programme was a successful raid against Genoa on the night of 22/23 October. Local reports mentioned the severe effect on the morale of the people of Genoa.

On the second strike of the programme, Bomber Command risked a daylight raid by 88 Lancasters on Milan, the second largest city in Italy, on 24 October. The raid came as a complete surprise in Milan, and damage was widespread.

49 That night, on 24/25 October, a further 71 aircraft of 1 and 3 Groups and the Pathfinders attacked Milan. Storms were encountered en route which dispersed the force. Some aircraft flew over neutral Switzerland and were warned off by anti-aircraft fire. Only 39 aircraft claimed to have bombed Milan, with minimal results. Three aircraft were lost.

Fraser's log book states, "Load: 5 x 500, 6 x 250, 13 x 5 flares." Fraser and his crew found 10/10 cloud over Milan, but fortunately their navigator, Flight Sergeant Coldwell, took a pinpoint while over Switzerland, so they bombed on the location established by dead reckoning from that pinpoint. Fraser then searched for 20 minutes to find the aiming point to fulfil his Pathfinder duties, but failing to find it, he brought the flares back to base.

On the return flight Fraser encountered some problems with the port-inner and starboard-outer engines. After crossing the Alps, he lost altitude

Stirlings bombers, believed to be returning from a raid on Genoa. To avoid identification, the squadron code has been deleted from the photograph.

and "ground defences near Paris fired when at 4000 feet." Fraser then crossed the French coast at 800 feet allowing Pilot Officer Cunningham to fire the tail guns at enemy defences.

For this long flight of 8:05 hours, Fraser had the added services of Sergeant Spain as second pilot, who at times took over the controls to give Fraser a break. Spain would accompany Fraser on other trips to Italy.

After the Milan raid, Fraser must have thought Cunningham and the other air gunners needed practice at firing on ground targets, because a few days later he took them for a practice over the Wash, letting them expend their ammunition at fixed targets on the water.

Target photograph taken over Genoa, 13/14 November 1942. The time-exposure photograph was taken automatically by a camera fitted to the belly of the aircraft. The white streaks are flares dropped from Fraser's bomber. Target photographs were used by intelligence staff to evaluate the results of raids.

50 Fraser's 50th operation was against Genoa on the night of 7/8 November. This would be the first of three consecutive raids to the same target. Out of a force of 175 aircraft on the night, including 39 Stirlings, six aircraft were lost. Fraser's log book recorded, "Load: 14 x 3 flares, 5 x 500, 4 x 250." The flares were dropped across the town, and the bombs dropped near the railway station on his second run. "Two photos obtained. Height 7500 feet." The flight time was 8:50 hours. It seems that weather conditions in the target area were perfect and the flights to and from the target were uneventful. Returning crews claimed a very successful and concentrated raid – and photographs confirmed this.

Fraser was invited to an investiture at Buckingham Palace on 10 November to receive his DFM from the King. Fraser wrote to his mother, "About a fortnight ago I went up to London to get the medal. I was allowed to take two with me." He took Mr and Mrs Ireland. Fraser didn't mention the occasion again as he believed all the details were in a letter to his mother from Mrs Ireland. Unfortunately, this letter doesn't exist today.

51 On the night of 13/14 November Fraser and his crew returned to Genoa for virtually a repeat of the previous raid. 67 Lancasters and nine Stirlings of the Pathfinder Force and 5 Group participated. No aircraft were lost. Fraser recorded, "Load: 18 x 3 flares, 2 x 1000 bombs. Flares dropped across town to north of harbour at zero + 5 [zero hour plus five minutes]." Their bombs were dropped near the aiming point and a photograph was taken from a height of 9000 feet. On their return across France the aircraft was holed by flak. Fraser's flight time was 8:10 hours. The raid was considered successful by Bomber Command.

52 Two nights later on 15/16 November, Fraser and his crew returned to Genoa for the third time in eight days. They were part of a force of 78 aircraft including 11 Stirlings. Again, no aircraft were lost. Apparently Fraser's Stirling arrived a tad early over the target, and while they were circling to use up time, the rear gunner, Jack Cunningham, spotted an Italian biplane fighter taking off below. After some quick words on the intercom, Fraser decided to give chase, but lost it after it carried out an evasive action – but not before Cunningham managed a few bursts in its direction. Using the four-engined Stirling as if it were a fighter aircraft was certainly uncharacteristic behaviour for any bomber pilot.

Fraser's log book mentions, "Load: 21 x 3 flares, 2 x 1000, 1 x 500. Flares dropped to north of AP [Aiming Point] at zero [on time]. Height: 9500 feet. Photo obtained." Fraser noticed that the flak was more accurate than on the previous two occasions. On the return flight he had to feather the port-inner propeller when near to base. Total flight time was 8:30 hours. Fraser pencilled his running total to date as 275 hours, a massive amount for any bomber pilot.

On the night of 18/19 November there was a raid on Turin, which Fraser and his crew did not participate in. No aircraft were lost, although a Halifax returned safely to England with just the pilot left aboard. Apparently while the aircraft was over the target area, flares ignited on board and the pilot ordered the crew to bale out, which they did. But amazingly, air rushing in the open escape hatch extinguished the flames!

53 The next operation for Fraser and his crew was a raid on Turin on the night of 20/21 November. It would be their first of three raids on the city over three weeks. This was a major raid on Italy with 232 aircraft, including 27 Stirlings, being dispatched. 10 aircraft were lost. The attack was considered successful – large fires were started, creating dense smoke over the target.

Fraser's bomb-load was "20 x 3 flares, 3 x 1000 bombs". There was a touch of déjà vu on this operation, similar to the raid on Genoa over a year previously when they ran out of fuel on their return to England. Fraser was informed by the flight engineer, "Lofty" Wade, that fuel consumption on the starboard-outer engine was excessive on the outbound flight. Fearing the possibility of not reaching home, Fraser immediately abandoned the operation and the bomb-load was dropped in a 'safe' zone over France. The troubled engine was then feathered, allowing the crew to return safely to Oakington on three engines, but only after experiencing accurate flak near Paris. Even though the flight was abandoned, their flight time was still 6:10 hours.

Even with four raids during November, and a busy schedule of training and test flights, Fraser managed some leave at the end of the month with the Irelands at Ambleside. In a letter to his mother at the time, he wrote, "I have now done 53 raids, and shall soon be coming off night bombing for good. I don't want to go back instructing if I can help it, so I'm going to try for fighters or intruders or something like that. I also think I could get back to New Zealand if I wanted to but I wouldn't like to leave England while the war is on as I would feel out of things." It seems Fraser was trying to pacify his mother who surely was worried about the amount of active flying he was doing. A second tour with Bomber Command normally consisted of 20 operations. He had 13 to go.

During November, Fraser was awarded his Pathfinder badge. It was a small brass eagle which was worn on the left breast pocket below his wings and DFM ribbon. Fraser had to pass a test and display suitable attributes to receive the coveted badge.

On the evening of 6 December, Fraser and his crew took off and climbed out over the North Sea, making their way to a raid on Mannheim. But just 20 minutes out, trouble developed with their starboard-inner engine, which had to be shut down and feathered. Their bomb-load was then jettisoned over the sea. At about the same time, a fire that had developed in the bomb compartment was quickly extinguished. They returned to Oakington after 80 minutes of flying.

As it happened, the raid was not a success because Mannheim was completely cloud-covered. The Pathfinders retained their flares and all bombing was done by dead-reckoning. Resulting damage was minimal. Out of 272 aircraft taking part, including 49 Stirlings, 10 were lost. 11 Stirlings were sent by 7 Squadron, of which only two claimed to have bombed the target. So it seems Fraser didn't miss out on any great excitement! The raid didn't count towards his operations tally, presumably because they didn't penetrate enemy airspace.

54 Three nights later, on 9/10 December, they headed back to Turin. It was a major raid with 227 aircraft taking part, including 25 Stirlings. Fraser's log book states, "Load: 21 x 3 flares. 3 x 1000 bombs. Town identified. Flares dropped near river [River Po or a tributary] and bombs in town." Fraser reported only moderate and inaccurate flak over the target, and heavy accurate flak over the French coast on their return. He didn't have a dedicated second pilot on this trip and after 7:40 hours at the controls he must have been exhausted.

Bomber Command records state that because of smoke over the city, the Pathfinders were not able to perform efficiently. However, the bombing effort was successful.

55 Fraser and his crew returned to Turin just two nights later on 11/12 December when 82 aircraft were sent on the raid. However, because severe icing conditions prevented many of them from gaining altitude over France, more than half of the force turned back

A visit by Bill Jordan (in civvies), New Zealand High Commissioner. Fraser is 3rd from left, front row.

before attempting to cross the Alps. Cloud tops were reported at 25,000 feet.

Only three 7 Squadron Stirlings, including Fraser's, set off from Oakington, each with a mixed bomb-load of "21 x 3 flares, 3 x 1000 bombs." Of the three, only Fraser's and one other crew made it to Turin.

Fraser said, "It was a filthy night. We decided to fly below the weather as long as we could, and then to climb quickly to get over the Alps and to rely on Coldwell's navigation. Everything worked well and we waited until Coldwell said, 'All right – come down.' We came down, all the crew holding their breath and praying that we weren't going to hit a mountain, and then suddenly we saw that we were just 20 miles north of Turin." It was exceptional navigation by Flight Sergeant Bob Coldwell. Fraser's log book entry stated, "Very bad weather throughout. Also icing. Crossed Alps blind. Broke cloud at target and identified town."

In an interview at the time, Fraser said, "We were surprised by the stiff opposition that we encountered, and hearing flak exploding uncomfortably near us. We flew right across the town and then circled and returned to drop our flares and bombs."

Just then, eight searchlights caught Fraser's Stirling in a cone for five minutes. However, it was their lucky night and they managed to get away. The other 7 Squadron Stirling that made it to Turin was spotted by Fraser's crew over the target before it was shot down.

Fraser's final line in his log book entry was, "Only aircraft from Squadron to reach target and return." Going by Bomber Command's summary of the raid, 28 crews claimed they bombed Turin, but reports from the city differ, stating that only three high-explosive bombs (two of them duds), and a few incendiaries or flares were identified. As Fraser's bomber was carrying three bombs and flares, it is reasonable to assume that his was the only aircraft to bomb Turin on the night! His flight time was 7:25 hours.

About this time, Mr Bill Jordan, High Commissioner for New Zealand in the United Kingdom, visited the Kiwis stationed at Oakington. Jordan had a reputation for knowing New Zealand servicemen personally and helping them with their many problems. Fraser wrote of the visit, "We had quite a long talk to him. He is a pretty decent old chap and he works very hard for the fellows. If ever we ask him to do anything for us, he does it if he possibly can."

56 Fraser's next operation was back to Germany on the night of 21/22 December. The target was the distant Munich, a flight of 7:50 hours. 137 aircraft were sent on the raid, with 12 being lost. About 110 crews claimed to have bombed Munich and started fires, but their photographs showed that all or most of the bombs fell in open country, possibly fooled by a decoy target.

Fraser wrote, "10/10 cloud at target. Load dropped on D.R. [dead-reckoning] from pinpoint."

The raid was an unforgettable one for Fraser and his crew, as they were pounced on by enemy fighters soon after leaving the target area. A contemporary newspaper article reported, "Another Stirling from the same squadron also fought two fighters. The rear gunner sighted a Messerschmitt off the port bow and gave it a burst. Then [an hour later] the second fighter, a Ju88, attacked from below and came up past the tail. The Stirling crew said they could hear thuds and bangs as shells exploded on the port wing." The mid-upper and rear turrets were knocked out in the burst.

Fraser (centre) and his crew beside a Stirling of 7 Squadron, Oakington, 1943. (l-r): PR Coldwell, unknown, unknown, Fraser, JW Roch, J Marshall, W Mayson.

Fraser took instant evasive action and dived his Stirling from 12,500 to 5000 feet, but the fighter was still there, firing into the starboard main plane. By this time Jack Cunningham in the rear turret "managed to get one gun going out of his four and drove it off" while Fraser dived a further 3000 feet. Between them they finally managed to shake it off. Meanwhile, a fire had started in the rear of the aircraft and the fuselage filled with fumes, but the wireless operator, Flight Sergeant Roch, and the flight engineer, Pilot Officer Robinson, miraculously put it out during the steep dive.

Fraser wrote home that the raid was "a bit on the warm side". The bomber was badly damaged. "A piece about a foot square was blown out of the left wing, three petrol tanks punctured, both gun turrets [mid-upper and rear] put out of action, the rear-gunner's parachute shot to ribbons, the petrol control wires shot away, the wireless aerial shot off, big holes all over the plane and a fire started in the rear."

The changeover petrol cocks for the tanks on the port side had also been severed. The tanks the aircraft was running on at the time had little petrol left, and there was no way to supplement them. But Robinson managed to connect up the tanks in time and get the petrol through.

The next problem for the crew was getting back to England. "The navigator lost all his stuff [during the evasive action] and couldn't tell where we were. However, we navigated from memory and got back home." But not before they found themselves flying over Luton with a big chimney sticking up higher than the aircraft! They shot up again, then when they were about to land found that one main wheel had not come down. Robinson again worked his magic, fixing it in time. The crew braced themselves for a crash, but the wheel held. Robinson was awarded the DFC for his efforts that night.

After touchdown, the relieved crew stood shivering on the wind-swept airfield waiting for a squadron truck to take them to debriefing and the hearty bacon and egg breakfast which would follow in the mess. They would then have fallen into bed, hoping for a couple of days to relax, and put the Munich experience behind them.

They all kept thinking the same thing: had Fraser delayed his evasive tactics by just a couple of seconds, the night-fighter would have sent them down in flames. It was only Fraser's skill and experience – and a cool head – that kept the crew alive. But most important of all was luck; when the crew looked at the aircraft the following day, they realised just how lucky they were.

Following the Munich raid, in which three 7 Squadron aircraft were lost, the squadron didn't fly operationally again until mid January 1943, partly because of bad weather, and partly because most of Bomber Command's raids over the New Year period were minor. The lull meant that crews could celebrate Christmas and enjoy a break from operations.

A new year with new targets

Fraser had an invitation to return to Ambleside for the festive season, but decided to stay close at Oakington. "We have had a pretty good time here and the weather was surprisingly good for this part of England. Christmas was quite sunny and it reminded me of New Zealand Christmases although it was a bit colder. We had dinner at night and it was pretty good for wartime and we even had turkey. On Christmas Eve most of us went into Cambridge and went to one of the big dances. On Christmas morning we were allowed to lie in bed for a change and of course I didn't say no to that."

An old RAF custom was followed on Christmas Day. "At midday all the officers and sergeants went to the airmen's mess and acted as waiters to the men and girls and served their Christmas dinner. We spent the afternoon quietly and at night the officers had their dinner. After that there was an all-ranks dance and then a stage show."

Celebrating the New Year was "pleasant although it wasn't anything like it was at Christmas." Fraser ended up seeing in the New Year with his crew in the Sergeants' Mess.

With the festive season over, Fraser started to concentrate on operations again. To keep his crew in shape, Fraser did 10 elementary training flights between the Munich raid and his first raid of 1943 in mid January.

Stirling N3641 of 7 Squadron, Oakington.

57 Fraser's first raid of the New Year was to Lorient on the night of 15/16 January. A raid on the target the previous night had been disappointing, so Bomber Command decided on a second strike the following night. Of the 157 aircraft sent on the raid, 40 were Stirlings. Two aircraft were lost. Surprisingly, 65 Wellingtons took part, which was a lot considering the type was soon to be retired from Main Force duties.

Bombing was more accurate than the previous night. Fraser's bombload was, "12 x 3 flares. 12 SBC [small bomb containers]. Target bombed at zero + 2." The target was seen clearly with only 3/10 cloud. The flak was only moderate. Members of the crew spotted a Me109 night fighter on their return but it did not attack. Fraser summed up the raid as, "quite a good trip and a fairly quiet time." His flight time was 4:50 hours.

During late 1942 a blind-bombing device, called *Oboe*, was fitted to some Bomber Command aircraft and controlled by two ground stations in England transmitting pulses. By receiving these pulses the aircraft would be guided over a target. But there were limits to the effective range of the device.

Hard on the heels of *Oboe* came a second blind-bombing device which had no limits to the range of its usefulness. This was *H2S*, the forerunner of the simple airborne ground-scanning radar set. In its early form, the flickering, often indeterminate picture was all that the *H2S* operator had; coastlines and wide rivers could usually be distinguished, city outlines sometimes, other features not often. But the device was a boon to a force which until then had to rely on dead-reckoning navigation and the *Gee* device. In the hands of a skilled operator, *H2S* proved to be an invaluable navigational aid.

The Pathfinder Force received the first *H2S* sets. 13 Stirlings of 7 Squadron and 10 Halifaxes of 35 Squadron had *H2S* sets installed and, following a training programme, they were ready for operational use by February 1943.

58 Fraser's crew, now trained in the use of *H2S*, was selected for a raid on Cologne on the night of 2/3 February. The bomber force comprised 161 aircraft, eight being Stirlings. Five aircraft were lost. Apart from two Mosquitoes carrying *Oboe*, the rest of the bomber force

February	1	Stirling	9255	Self	Crew 08'	Air Test T
February	2	Stirling	9255	Self	Crew	Air Test
February	2	Stirling	9255	Self	P/o. Roch	58 Raid on Cologne. Warning flare
				Sgt Tomlinson	P/o. Caldwell	dropped at zero. Aircraft then coned by 30-50
					P/o. Marshall	s/mins & held for 15 minutes. In evasive action height
					P/o. Cunningham	reduced from 18000' to 10000'. Second run made at
					Sgt. Maysen	this height & T.I.s dropped. Compasses u/s &
					F/sgt. Turner	came out Ostend. Heavy accurate flak here and
						at Target

GRAND TOTAL [Cols. (1) to (10)].
848 Hrs. **15** Mins.
TOTALS CARRIED FORWARD

Log book entry for the raid on Cologne, 2/3 February 1943. The recommendation for an award to Fraser Barron by Wing Commander Donaldson was based on this raid.

were four-engined aircraft. In the cloudy conditions over the target, the results were disappointing – no clear concentration of markers was achieved and subsequent bombing was scattered.

Unfortunately, a 7 Squadron Pathfinder Stirling was shot down over Holland, allowing the Germans to obtain a *H2S* set on only the second night the device was used.

Fraser had his own drama on the night – coned by 30-50 searchlights, he defied the ground defences while he completed his run. He later stated, "In a few minutes the anti-aircraft batteries opened fire, and one of the airscrew blades was damaged and the rear-gunner's turret smashed. Although I tried every method of evasive action to escape from the searchlights, they still held us in their glare. They lit up the Stirling for 15 minutes. Then we managed to escape from them by diving away from the target after releasing our bombs."

In the evasive action they dropped from 18,000 to 10,000 feet. On the return flight the Stirling, with its compasses now out of order, crossed the Belgium coast at Ostend where they encountered more heavy flak, but they reached their base without further damage. The action-packed flight took four hours.

Afterwards, Fraser realised just how near he was to being killed. "I really thought they had me that night."

59 There was to be no rest for Fraser and his crew, as they were sent to bomb Hamburg the very next night, 3/4 February. 263 aircraft were dispatched, including 66 Stirlings. 16 aircraft were lost, including eight Stirlings. This high Stirling loss was attributed to the

aircraft's low ceiling – especially in icy conditions – making them more vulnerable to flak. Not only did icing conditions in cloud over the North Sea cause many of the aircraft to abandon the raid, but the Pathfinders were also unable to produce concentrated target marking, causing the Main Force bombing to be scattered. Overall, the results were disappointing.

Fraser was in for more misfortune on this raid. Only 20 miles from the target the port-outer engine failed. As a result his Stirling lost height quickly, so he abandoned the operation and released his bomb-load. Still unable to gain sufficient height, the aircraft flew right into a storm, and icing conditions became so bad that it lost further height until it was only 2000 feet above the ground.

"Things were so bad that night that I thought they had got me again. I very nearly had to do a crash-landing in Holland and for about a quarter of an hour it was touch and go." Fraser fought to keep the aircraft speed above its 105 miles-per-hour stalling speed.

"However, luck has always been on my side since I've been over here." Suddenly, over Rotterdam, the Stirling entered a rain-storm, and in a few minutes the ice was melting, and the aircraft gradually gained height. Fraser nursed the Stirling up to 4000 feet, and completed the remainder of the flight safely. His flight time for this raid is unknown as a summary sticker had been placed over the figures in his log book.

The two previous raids made Fraser reflect on his mortality and the importance of teamwork and morale in his crew. He had the highest respect for his crew. "They always stuck with me in the worst of times and I knew they would never let me down. The only thing I was frightened of was that one day I might let them down and not be able to bring them home."

On 8 February it was announced that Fraser had been awarded the DFC. The Official Citation reads: "As captain of an aircraft, Flight Lieutenant Barron has evinced a high order of courage and skill, together with determination to strike at the enemy on every possible occasion and with the greatest destructive effect. Throughout, he has given evidence of keenness and tenacity in accomplishing his allotted tasks and on many occasions has displayed a complete disregard for his personal safety."

The awarding of the DFC was considered a 'general' award as no specific action was mentioned in the citation.

After the award, Fraser merely wrote home, "I got the DFC a couple of days ago, but I suppose you know about that by now."

60 On the night of 11/12 February, Fraser and his crew were hoping for a smooth operation against Wilhelmshaven. 177 aircraft were sent to the target, 8 of them Stirlings. Three aircraft were lost.

On the outbound trip Fraser had trouble with the starboard-outer oil cooler. When he and the other Pathfinders found that the target area was completely covered in cloud, they used *H2S* for sky-marking with parachute flares. Fraser's log book states, "Flak moderate and inaccurate. Sky-marking flares were dropped at zero + 10. Height 16,000 feet."

The marking was carried out with great accuracy and the Main Force bombing was extremely effective. Through the clouds crews saw a huge explosion on the ground as a naval ammunition depot blew up. The resulting explosion devastated an area of 120 acres and caused widespread damage to the naval dockyard and nearby town.

The *H2S* was probably effective on the night because set operators could easily pick up the harbour outline. The raid represented the first blind-bombing success of the *H2S* radar device.

Fraser and his crew must have been relieved to notch up a successful raid without another crisis. After the recent Munich and Hamburg raids, this must have seemed a 'milk run'.

61 On the night of 14/15 February, it was back to Cologne. Fraser would be hoping for no repeat of his last visit. On the night 243 aircraft took part, nine of these being Stirlings. Nine aircraft were lost.

As there was 10/10 cloud over the target, the Pathfinder marking was again based on the sky-markers dropped with the help of *H2S*, but the operation was only of limited success. Fraser wrote, "Bombed zero + 2. Heavy flak in barrage but not too accurate."

While pulling away from the target they were jumped by a night fighter. Fraser took violent evasive action, and after dropping some

Fraser's crew during his second tour in front of Stirling G for George of 7 Squadron, Oakington. (l-r): Unknown, PR Coldwell, unknown, JW Roch, J Marshall, Fraser and W Mayson.

distance, he managed to lose it.

They were in the same aircraft (9255) with the same engine that had given them trouble on the previous raid. It gave them trouble again. On their return Fraser had to feather the starboard-outer propeller and finish the trip on three engines. As well as that, the throttle Exactor burst and forced them to land at Waterbeach. Fraser returned the Stirling to Oakington two days later, after repairs were completed.

Unbeknown to Fraser at the time, the raid was to be his last operation in a Stirling. Apparently, his second tour was over. He was preparing for his next operation when the Wing Commander sprang the order on him.

Fraser was taken off operational duties on 2 March, the same day he was awarded the DSO. It was an 'immediate' award granted for an immediate act of bravery. At the time Fraser was the first New Zealander to be awarded the trio of decorations. The citation was based on the recommendation written by Wing Commander Donaldson, the Commanding Officer of 7 Squadron.

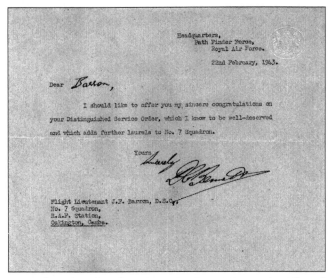

Congratulatory letter from Group Captain Don Bennett, Commanding Officer of the Pathfinder Force.

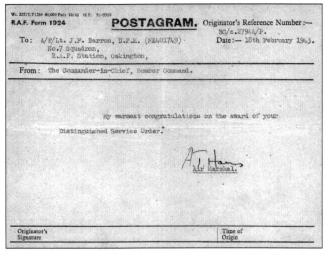

Congratulatory postagram from Air Marshal Harris, Commanding Officer of Bomber Command.

The Official Citation for the DSO reads: "One night in February, 1943, this officer was the captain of an aircraft detailed to attack Cologne. When nearing the target area his aircraft was held in a cone of searchlights and subjected to heavy fire from the ground defences. Despite this, Flight Lieutenant Barron remained on his course, defying an intense and concentrated barrage, and pressed home a successful attack on his second run over the target. This officer displayed exceptional gallantry and devotion to duty, setting an example of the highest order."

The recommendation, dated 15 February, was based on the recent Cologne raid on the night of 2/3 February. After giving a full account of what happened on the night, Donaldson finished by writing, "Barron has consistently shown himself to be a very cool and courageous captain who presses home his attacks with vigour and a determination that are truly magnificent."

In a letter to his mother, "Word came through that I had got the DSO ... I can tell you that I almost fainted when I heard. I knew that I was up for another award of some sort and thought it would be a Bar to the DFC, and didn't for a minute think it would be the other. It is usually given to officers of higher rank such as Wing Commanders and Colonels." For once Fraser showed he was proud about his awards. "The three ribbons under my wings look quite a row."

Fraser was sad to be leaving his mates and home at Oakington. "I was very sorry to leave the squadron and operational life. I did 61 raids altogether and was about to do the 62nd when the Wing Commander told me the Chief of Bomber Command [Harris] said I had done enough and wasn't allowed to do any more." Forever thinking about the welfare of his crew, "I was hoping to be allowed to do another to finish my crew off but there was nothing doing."

Fraser had completed 15 raids with 7 Squadron, and adding to this the further seven completed with 1651 HCU, his total since his first tour was 22, two more than the requisite 20 operations. Wing Commander Donaldson's final assessment of Fraser as a heavy bomber pilot, pasted into his log book, "Above the Average," which is high praise indeed for a young 22-year-old pilot from New Zealand.

There must have been some sighs of relief back in New Zealand when the news of his new posting arrived. His parents would have been wondering just how long Fraser's luck could hold out before he was lost over Europe.

The prospect that he might be grounded from operations for a couple of years meant the war could be over before he was allowed to return to front-line duties. They were not only proud of their son, but for once were comforted by the thought he would come home.

Fraser didn't convey to his family that he need never return to operations again. Airmen who had completed two operational tours could not be ordered back onto front-line duties.

But Fraser clearly did not intend to spend the rest of the war as an instructor or stuck behind some desk. He wanted to be at the front where all the action and excitement was – doing his bit for King and country.

7 Squadron's S for Sugar banks away over England.

Away from the action

After Fraser was taken off operations, he had a few weeks' leave with the Irelands at Ambleside before being posted to 16 OTU based at RAF Upper Heyford, Oxfordshire, to complete an instructor's course. While there Fraser was back behind the controls of the trusty Wellington. The course took less than two weeks and included 9:30 hours of flying. On the last day he managed to do 45 minutes of aerobatics in a Tiger Moth along with Squadron Leader Lyster. During his short stay at Upper Heyford, Fraser was promoted to Squadron Leader on 7 March 1943.

Fraser's next posting was to 11 OTU at RAF Westcott, northwest of London in Buckinghamshire, with instructor's duties starting in earnest on 16 March. He was put in command of C Flight. All instructor's flights were in Wellington 1Cs, the early Wellington operational type. Flights were similar to those at Waterbeach – cross-country flights, night flying tests (some done in daylight), circuits and landings, air tests and night landings. To break the boredom Fraser would take a station-based Tiger Moth and hop across to Oakington to catch up with friends.

Soon after Fraser's arrival at Westcott, a position became available for a gunnery instructor. Fraser got to work and after pulling some strings, managed to get Jack Cunningham for the position. So Fraser took a Wellington on 20 March and flew to Oakington for lunch, then on to Waterbeach to collect Jack, then home to Westcott. He even took along Flight Sergeant Walters, a fellow Kiwi, as second pilot.

Being stationed at Westcott was never going to be a holiday for Fraser; he held a responsible position and was kept active on flying duties. "The work is quite hard and very different from anything I've been used to on operations, but I'm finding it very interesting so far. All the chaps here are a very decent crowd. The Wing Commander and Group Captain are both first-class men and that's a big thing on a station like this."

On 25 May Fraser was invited to an investiture at Buckingham Palace to receive the DFC and DSO. Mrs Ireland was in attendance on the day

Dignitaries visit an Air Force base, 1943. Fraser is 5th from right in the second row.

and the two stayed over in London for a few days. Fraser was presented with both decorations by the King. Mrs Ireland wrote in a letter to Fraser's parents, "Fraser was among the first to be decorated. He came immediately behind six generals. The King was in naval uniform and looked much better than the last time I saw him. He said a few words to Fraser, shook him by the hand, then, as Fraser walked away with the medals [pinned to his breast], they jangled, and he put a hand over them. It was such a boyish gesture. He did look nice. We were at the palace about two hours." Fraser then lunched with Bill Jordan and his wife at the New Zealand Forces Club.

Afterwards, Bill Jordan also penned a letter to Fraser's parents, "Last week I had the great pleasure of meeting and having lunch with your son, Fraser. What a fine lad he is. I am sure you are very proud of him, and I assure you that he is held in real affection by those with whom he is associated. He has just received the DFC and DSO from the King. Fraser is certainly one of New Zealand's most distinguished sons. We trust that all will go well with him and that he will return safely to you."

Both Mrs Ireland and Bill Jordan made comments about Fraser's youthfulness. Fraser, a Squadron Leader who had been decorated three times, was still perceived as a young man.

As time went on, Fraser noticed he was spending more time in administration than in the pilot's seat. "It's one o'clock in the morning. We have got some crews out on cross-countries and I am waiting up for them to come back. Last night I went on a cross-country flight myself with one of the crews, but I found it very tame after Germany. I don't do much flying now as most of my work is sitting behind a desk in an office and I'm lucky if I can get up in the air more than once a week."

This last comment by Fraser was an exaggeration, because skimming his log book reveals that Fraser did 14 flights in April, 17 in May, 16 in June, 22 in July, 16 in August, 24 in September, 33 in October, etc. If anything, his flying duties were increasing! Maybe as time went on he was becoming more frustrated and hemmed in with the drudgery and boredom of an instructor's life. Other instructors would probably warm to the OTU life – all Fraser wanted was to get his name back on the active list.

Also, according to his log book, Fraser made numerous cross-country flights to Oakington, staying overnight on some occasions. Obviously it was important to Fraser to keep in touch with the scene at his old base, in the hope that he would be posted back there some day.

Apart from flying and administration duties, Fraser turned his hand to

Fraser dines with Bill Jordan, High Commissioner of New Zealand, and Mrs Jordan, after being presented with the DFC and DSO, 25 May 1943.

Mr and Mrs Bill Jordan and Fraser (front left), with New Zealand servicemen in front of the New Zealand Forces Club, London, 25 May 1943, after his investiture.

public relations. As a highly-decorated airman, he was much in demand for speaking to help maintain enthusiasm amongst newly-recruited airmen; there were visits and talks with operational crews, and lectures on tactics. There were also photographic sessions – on 21 June Fraser was photographed with two Maori pupils then passing through 11 OTU.

Fraser continued to take leave, enjoying a week at Ambleside in both June and August. For the August visit his friend Bill Black accompanied him. Mrs Ireland enjoyed the visits, writing to Fraser's parents, "I miss him very much, but I am so glad he is out of operations. I can sleep much better. I keep telling him he is of more value imparting his knowledge to others than going out himself ... Mr Ireland and I think of him as our adopted son for the time being."

But Fraser's heart still lay with operations. He expressed his eagerness in a letter home during November. "By the way, I may be going back on operations with the Pathfinders in the near future. I've been applying pressure in the right place for about three months to get back and am hoping something will come of it soon. I've been told that I'll be able to do only another 20 raids and no more. A lot of chaps have offered to go

Map reading instruction at 11 OTU. Fraser instructs New Zealanders Tame Waera (wearing flying harness in left photograph) and Charles Pinker.

Fraser (centre of middle row), at 11 OTU, Westcott, 1943.

back with me so I won't have any trouble getting a crew." The "right place" he referred to was Hamish Mahaddie.

Fraser volunteered on a couple of occasions to fly a Wellington close to the German coast looking for ditched crews. "I went to the German coast in daylight to look for crews that had landed in the sea, but I didn't find anything and didn't meet any opposition. But it was a break from the usual routine." These two searches took place on 23 May (3:45 hours) and 1 October (5:15 hours). To Fraser it was the closest thing to going on a raid without actually going on a raid!

During September and October the quality of the meals presented in the officers' mess fell off in quality, leading to a new messing officer being appointed. Fraser wrote, "So far he has been pretty good. It is going to be great here after the war when we can eat what we want to and buy anything we like from the shops." As it happened, some rationing in Britain continued after the war into the 1950s. "It must be great in New Zealand not to be rationed very much and still get things like apples and pears easily. Over here we get enough to eat and I suppose we are getting the right kind of things to eat but it is always plain and we rarely get luxuries like steak and chicken." Fraser didn't mention the steady flow of parcels he received from home containing cakes, shortbread, biscuits, sweets, fruit, chewing gum and canned oysters.

At the beginning of November, Fraser took another week of leave at Ambleside. While there he tried to catch up on sleep but didn't overlook the cinema, church and social activities.

Fraser's last logged instructor's flight was on 23 December, in a Wellington X with Sergeant Cooper as second pilot, for a duration of 30 minutes. Four days later, after celebrating Christmas at Westcott, he flew to Oakington to rejoin 7 Squadron. He had been personally sanctioned to return to operations.

Fraser's third and final tour was to be strictly limited to just 20 operations, meaning his final tally would finish at 81.

Third tour – "a piece of cake"

For his third and final tour, Fraser hand-picked his new crew. "I have a very good and experienced crew with me and I think it will be even better than last time."

With him when he arrived at Oakington on 27 December 1943, were: Pilot Officer Jack Walters, Kiwi and wireless operator; Pilot Officer Bob Weatherall DFM, Canadian and air gunner; Warrant Officer Albert Price, Englishman and bomb aimer; Flight Lieutenant Bob Coldwell DSO, DFM, Yorkshireman and navigator, having previously flown with Fraser; Flight Sergeant Joe Lamonby, Englishman and air gunner; and Sergeant Lofty Johnson, Englishman from Newcastle and flight engineer.

Many changes and improvements had happened in Fraser's absence. These were mostly in aircraft types, navigation and bombing aids, pyrotechnics, tactics and methods. The crew had to become familiar with Window – strips of aluminium foil jettisoned in volume from aircraft to cloud or jam enemy radar. There were also improvements to TIs (target indicators) – a type of marker flare available in different colours. One thing that hadn't changed at Oakington – Squadron Leader Hamish Mahaddie was still with the squadron, only now he was the Pathfinders' training inspector and recruiter. He described himself as Bennett's 'horse thief,' pinching the best crews from Main Force squadrons.

But the biggest change for Fraser and his crew was in the type of aircraft. From May 1943, 7 Squadron had re-equipped with Lancasters (Mk III). Their first conversion flight was on 2 January 1944, with Fraser in the second pilot seat. That same day, Fraser captained a solo landing flight, which was a take off, half-circuit of the aerodrome and landing taking just 10 minutes. From then on, Fraser would always be in the pilot seat. He wrote home, "I'm flying Lancasters this time and they are really wonderful aeroplanes. I like them even more than the Stirlings." After four more training flights they were ready for some action, which

Arriving back from a raid. Using inboard engines only, Lancasters taxi back to their dispersals. Small groups of ground crew await the bombers' return no matter what hour or weather.

finally came on the night of 5/6 January.

The raid was on Stettin, involving 348 Lancasters and 10 Halifaxes. No Stirlings or Wellingtons took part. Disappointingly, while flying over Denmark, the oxygen supply in Fraser's aircraft failed, forcing them to abandon the operation. "The target was Stettin but I had to turn back after getting about two thirds of the way there as all my oxygen failed. I was very disappointed but better luck next time."

This raid wasn't added to Fraser's tally of 61, even after a flight time of 5:45 hours. Fraser had abandoned raids of much shorter duration in the past, but they were still added to his total. One would surmise that since Fraser had only 20 raids left before retirement from operations he wanted each and every one of them to be the real thing, so he may have contrived the operation not to be added to his tally.

62 Fraser's first genuine operation in a Lancaster and in his third tour happened on the night of 14/15 January, in a raid on Brunswick. A massive total of 496 Lancasters and two Halifaxes took part. The Pathfinders contributed 58 aircraft to the raid. German fighters

closed on the bomber stream soon after it crossed the German frontier near Bremen, and scored steadily until the Dutch coast was crossed on the return flight. 38 Lancasters were lost. Unfortunately, 11 of those were Pathfinders.

Most of the attack fell either in the countryside or in Wolfenbüttel and other small towns to the south of Brunswick.

Fraser's log book states, "Load: 1 x 4000, 6 x 1000, TIs, Flares." Their *H2S* radar set was unserviceable so they joined the Main Force to bomb. "Little opposition. Bombed from 20,500 feet. Good trip." Fraser's crew

Avro Lancaster

The Avro Lancaster was a four-engined heavy bomber and mainstay of the RAF in the latter years of the war.

The "Lanc" became the most famous and most successful of the Second World War night bombers, delivering 608,612 tons of bombs in 156,000 sorties.

Although the Lancaster was primarily a night bomber, it excelled in many other roles including daylight precision bombing, and gained worldwide renown as the 'Dambuster' used in the 1943 raids on Germany's Ruhr Valley dams.

A total of 7377 Lancasters were built. In the four years of combat service, 3249 were lost in action and another 487 were destroyed or damaged while on the ground. Only 24 Lancasters completed more than 100 successful missions.

Demand for the Rolls Royce Merlin engine constantly threatened to outstrip supply in Britain. One solution was the manufacture of Merlin engines by the Packard motor company in the USA. These Packard Merlins were used in a variety of aircraft, but perhaps the biggest consumer was the Lancaster III, of which 3039 were built (requiring over 12,000 engines). The Packard Merlin delivered 1420hp at takeoff.

Specifications (Mk III)

Length:	69ft 4in (21.08m)
Wingspan:	102ft (31m)
Maximum speed:	287mph (462kph)
Cruising speed:	200mph (322kph)
Ceiling:	24,700ft (5793m)
Range:	2530 miles (4072km) with 7000lb (3178kg) bomb-load
Engines:	Four Packard Merlin V12 20, 22, or 24, of 1420hp each
Payload:	Up to 22,000lb (9988kg)
Armament:	2 x .303 machine guns in nose turret, 2 x .303 machine guns in mid-upper turret and 4 in tail turret
Crew:	7

was lucky not to be intercepted by a night fighter – unlike many other bombers on the night. While approaching England on their return, Fraser was diverted to Westcott. His flight time was 5:45 hours.

The Lancaster was a vastly-superior aircraft to the Stirling, with a huge bomb-load, a capacious bomb bay, and a ceiling of over 24,000 feet. On this raid Fraser's bomb-load was much bigger than on any previous raid. It was the first time his aircraft had carried a 4000-pound bomb, and he was able to fly over the target at a much higher altitude, making him less vulnerable to flak.

Fraser wrote home excited about the raid. "I suppose I was lucky because I had a very easy trip and also a successful one. It was the first time I had been over Germany for nearly a year and I felt a bit scared crossing the enemy coast and seeing the flak and searchlights again. But once I got well into Germany I settled down again. The old place hasn't changed much." The reference to being scared is the first time Fraser had admitted to being frightened while on operations.

In the same letter Fraser mentioned his concerns about a tour of just 20 operations being too short. "They are going to let me do only 20 raids on this tour and at the rate they have been bombing lately, it won't take

The Lancaster's functional 'office' with the pilot's position on the left and flight engineer on the right.

long unfortunately." So the hunger for excitement and action was still there.

63 Fraser's next raid was on the night of 20/21 January. Berlin was the target. The raid was the 12th major attack on the capital in just 10 weeks. It was a biggie. The force comprised 769 aircraft – 495 Lancasters, 264 Halifaxes and 10 Mosquitoes. 35 aircraft were lost. Most of the bombers departed England in the last of the daylight as zero hour over the target was 19:35 hours. New routing tactics were used by Bomber Command in an effort to reduce losses experienced previously on the straight-in route to the target. Although the new route took a wide swing to the north, it wasn't enough to confuse the Germans. Night fighters were amongst them early and scored steadily until the force was well on the way home. The heavy cloud over Germany was a blessing for the bombers – clearer weather conditions would have resulted in more night fighters in the air, and subsequently, more losses.

Fraser's bomb-load was, "1 x 4000. 4 x 1000. TIs." He commented, "Wizard trip. 9/10 cloud over target. Good run on 'Y' [*H2S*]. Opposition slight on route and at target." Still their luck held out, sighting no night fighters throughout the operation.

First Bomber Command reports indicate that most of the bombs fell on eastern districts of Berlin. But since no photographic reconnaissance was possible over the target until a further four raids on Berlin took place, an accurate report was impossible.

64 Magdeburg was the target of Fraser's 64th operation, on the night of 21/22 January, the very next night after the Berlin raid. Bomber Harris was playing mind games with the German defences – he gave every impression that the raid would be on Berlin, but diverted to Magdeburg, west of Berlin, at the last moment. The German night-fighter controllers were a bit slow realising the final target, but this did not give the Allies an advantage, as most of the fighters were able to stay with the bomber stream.

The force consisted of 648 aircraft, including 421 Lancasters, 224 Halifaxes and three Mosquitoes. Losses were 57 aircraft including 25 Halifaxes. Probably three quarters of the losses were caused by night

A typical 'tactical' target bomb-load in the Lancaster's capacious bomb bay. A 4000-pound 'cookie' is surrounded by 500- and 250-pounders.

fighters. Clearly the Halifaxes, particularly the Mk II and Mk V, were not up to the task, although they were not removed from the Main Force until after the operation against Leipzig on 19/20 February.

Fraser was carrying one 4000-pounder, five 1000-pounders, target indicators and flares. His only comments about the raid were, "Good trip. Fairly clear over target. Bombed zero + 10. Opposition slight. Heavy near coast." Still no contact with night fighters. His flight time of 6:40 hours reflected the longer diversion route taken on the outward journey.

Despite all the excitement of raids over Germany, the war wasn't foremost in Fraser's mind. He was in love. In a letter to his mother dated 26 January, Fraser spilled the news of the existence of a woman in his life. What probably prompted him was the announcement of his sister Patsy's engagement. "I'll bet you have been worrying your head that I'll get married over here. Well, I've never had a great deal of time to worry about girls since I've been in the Air Force and anyway, I've always been too interested in flying and operations."

Like a bomber over its target, Fraser was circling the subject somewhat. "But, when I was instructing, I met a girl I liked very much. This was

Fraser on leave relaxing with friends.

about 10 months ago and I've been friendly ever since. She was a Waaf [Women's Auxiliary Air Force] at the camp and we used to see quite a lot of each other on duty.

"I used to take her out now and again and now that I'm back on operations I don't see her very much although we write to each other."

Fraser didn't want his mother to think that a wedding was imminent – "For goodness sake don't start jumping to conclusions that I'm engaged or anything like that because I'm not (yet)" – but still wanted his mother to know that he was serious by adding the "yet" in brackets.

Her name was Marie. She was a month older than Fraser and her home was London.

Obviously Fraser made a choice of either going back on operations or staying in an instructor's role close to Marie. Unfortunately for Marie, the lure of the bombers won! But Fraser did organise an elaborate system of sending a telegram after each raid through a third person, so that Marie didn't worry unduly about him.

65 Fraser returned to Berlin on the night of 30/31 January. A force of 534 aircraft made up of 440 Lancasters, 82 Halifaxes and 12 Mosquitoes flew a direct line to Berlin, and attempts by the German night-fighter controllers to intercept the bomber stream over the sea

failed. The bombers were therefore well on their way to Berlin before meeting any night fighters, but the Germans were then able to follow them until well into their return flight. 33 aircraft were lost.

The raid was through solid cloud-cover but Bomber Command was still able to claim a concentrated attack. There was heavy bombing in the city as well as widespread bombing in surrounding country areas.

Fraser's *H2S* radar was again unserviceable, otherwise, according to him, it was a "good trip. Opposition slight." They dropped one 4000-pounder, four 1000-pounders, target indicators and flares over the target. Fraser's flight time was 6:20 hours, and his running total to date is pencilled at 359:15 hours.

66 After two weeks of training flights — mostly testing and improving their skills with the *H2S* radar — Fraser and his crew were sent back to Berlin on the night of 15/16 February. On this raid a double bluff was planned — 16 Mosquitoes were to precede the Pathfinders dropping spoof route markers, TIs, bombs and fighter flares in the Berlin area, hoping this would deceive the defenders into thinking that Berlin

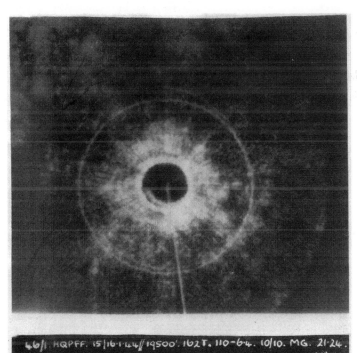

H2S target-marking photograph of raid on Berlin, 15/16 February 1944 (wrongly marked January).

Bombing up a Lancaster, preparing it for the night's raid.

was a minor raid and not the main target on the night. In addition, 24 Lancasters would carry out a diversionary attack on railways at Frankfurt-on-Oder, some 50 miles east of Berlin.

Despite all the diversions, the main bomber force was still identified while crossing the North Sea, and German fighters harried it all the way to the target and, against instructions, attacked the bombers over Berlin.

891 aircraft were dispatched – 561 Lancasters, 314 Halifaxes and 16 Mosquitoes. This was the largest force sent to Berlin, and outside the 1000-bomber raids, the biggest force sent to any target. The quantity of bombs, 2642 tons, was a record. Losses were 43 aircraft. Damage to Berlin was extensive with 599 large and 572 medium fires, and nearly 1000 houses and 526 of the large number of temporary wooden barracks destroyed.

This raid would bring an end to the 'Battle of Berlin,' with only one more raid to take place on the city in this period, and that still a month off. However, Mosquitoes would continue to plague the city.

As usual, Fraser carried one 4000-pounder, two 1000-pounders, target indicators and flares. He recorded in his log book, "Flak more intense and accurate than formerly. More flak on route." The raid took Fraser seven hours. 7 Squadron suffered heavily on the night with four aircraft lost out of 23 dispatched.

As a consequence of 7 Squadron losing four aircraft over Berlin, Fraser was promoted to Wing Commander, taking command of A Flight of the three-flight squadron. It was effective from the earlier date of 12 February. As before, a modest letter would go home, "I almost forgot to tell you, I've been promoted again – I'm now a wing commander. I never thought I should ever get as high as that." The rank is equivalent to lieutenant colonel in the army. Fraser had risen from Sergeant to Wing Commander in less than three years.

67 Four nights later, on 19/20 February, Fraser and his crew were dispatched to bomb Leipzig. The large bomber force of 823 aircraft, comprising 561 Lancasters, 255 Halifaxes and seven Mosquitoes, was sent on what was to be an unhappy raid for Bomber Command. Losses on the raid were 78 aircraft – 44 Lancasters and 34 Halifaxes. A further three crashed in England. One other aircraft was lost in a diversion operation to Berlin. Of the total Bomber Command effort on the night, 79 aircraft were lost. This was the heaviest Bomber Command loss of the war so far. As a result of the raid, Halifax IIs and Vs were permanently withdrawn from operations to Germany.

The bomber force was attacked by night fighters all the way to the target area. Because of strong, unexpected wind on the night, many bombers arrived early over the target area, so had to orbit and await the Pathfinders. Four aircraft were lost to collisions and 20 were shot down by flak. Leipzig was cloud-covered, so Pathfinders had to use sky-marking. The raid appeared to be concentrated in its early stages, but scattered later. Fighters further harassed the force coming away from Leipzig.

Fraser's bomb-load was again one 4000-pounder, two 1000-pounders, target indicators and flares – the same as his previous raid. He stoically commented in his log book, "Accurate flak and many fighter flares on route out. Many combats and many aircraft seen falling. A successful but tough trip." His flight time was 6:45 hours.

Fraser showed his feelings about the Leipzig raid in a letter home, "The Leipzig trip was the only one I didn't enjoy very much. We lost 79 of our bombers. There were hundreds of night fighters up against us and it was pretty solid going all the way. Luckily I've got a wonderful crew."

Miraculously, Fraser's crew hadn't engaged one enemy fighter during the six completed raids of their tour so far.

7 Squadron lost a further two aircraft on the raid, making it six crews in just two consecutive raids. At the time the squadron worked on 11 crews per flight, making a total squadron strength of 33 crews. The loss of six crews equated to 18%. Before the end of February the squadron would participate in three further raids on Stuttgart, Schweinfurt and Augsburg, not losing any further crews. Fraser would fly in them all.

68 Fraser's next raid was against Stuttgart in southern Germany on the night of 20/21 February. It was another major raid with 598 aircraft dispatched, including 460 Lancasters, 126 Halifaxes and 12 Mosquitoes. For once the losses were minimal with nine bombers lost. A North Sea sweep and a diversion raid on Munich successfully drew German fighters away from the Main Force. The target was cloud-covered and the bombing became scattered. Considerable damage was reported to the centre of the city.

Fraser's bomb-load was exactly the same as the previous two raids. For the first time on this tour their aircraft was attacked by a night fighter. It happened just after completing their bombing run. Fortunately, the night fighter was spotted in time by the alert crew, and following some quick evasive action by Fraser, they lost it. Otherwise, it was a "very quiet trip". Flight time was 6:40 hours.

Between the previous three raids there wasn't one training flight, and another two raids would be completed before any more took place. The men were probably too exhausted for anything else but operations.

A Lancaster starting up at night.

69 On the night of 24/25 February, Fraser and his crew bombed Schweinfurt, east of Frankfurt. 734 aircraft, including 554 Lancasters, 169 Halifaxes and 11 Mosquitoes, attacked the target, home of Germany's main ball-bearing factories. 33 aircraft were lost. 266 American B-17s had hit the target the afternoon of the previous day with disappointing results, so the target needed revisiting. Bomber Command introduced a new tactic on the night – the force was split into two parts separated by a two-hour interval. The first wave of 392 aircraft lost 22 and the second wave of 342 lost 11. Schweinfurt later reported only 'nominal damage'.

Fraser was with the first wave. His bomb-load was similar to recent raids – one 4000-pounder, three 1000-pounders, target indicators and flares. Zero hour was 23:05. Fraser was nine minutes late in bombing, but "had a good run on target which was clear. Many searchlights and moderate flak." His flight time was 6:50 hours.

The results of the first wave were not good. Despite the favourable bombing conditions, of the 338 crews who claimed to have attacked, only seven aircraft brought back photographs centred on the target area. Another 117 photographs were within a three-mile radius and a further 268 were plotted outside the designated area. The results were clearly not as good as Bomber Command had hoped.

70 The next night of 25/26 February, Fraser and his crew attacked Augsburg, just northwest of Munich. It was Bomber Command's first raid on this target. 594 aircraft took part including 461 Lancasters, 123 Halifaxes and 10 Mosquitoes. The various diversions and the splitting of the Main Force helped reduce casualties still further than at Schweinfurt. Losses were 21 aircraft.

Fraser was in the second wave this time. Again, his bomb-load was similar to recent raids – one 4000-pounder, four 1000-pounders, target indicators and flares. Their *H2S* became unserviceable only eight minutes from the target, so they bombed visually. Fraser recorded, "Large fires. Moderate opposition." His flight time was 6:30 hours.

Overall, the raid was outstandingly successful, which is surprising considering tactics and conditions were similar to the previous night. The beautiful old centre of Augsburg was completely destroyed. About 3000 homes were destroyed and 5000 damaged, and up to 90,000 people were bombed out. The Germans publicised the raid as an extreme example of 'terror bombing'.

During February, in spite of his busy schedule, Fraser still managed to make time for Marie. They spent a 48-hour pass together in London. A show they attended was interrupted by a small Luftwaffe raid: "The Jerries came over and dropped a few bombs and although there were one or two fires in the city, I don't think they did much damage."

71 On the night of 1/2 March, the target was Stuttgart again. 557 aircraft were dispatched to the raid, including 415 Lancasters, 129 Halifaxes and 13 Mosquitoes, with only four aircraft being lost. The low losses were due to thick cloud on the routes to and from the target, making it difficult for the German fighters to make contact. Over the target the Pathfinders' markers quickly disappeared into the cloud below.

It was difficult to ascertain the amount of damage on the night, but local reports showed that there was extensive damage to the central, western and northern parts of Stuttgart. Several important industrial premises were seriously damaged, including the Bosch works and the Daimler-Benz motor factory.

Fraser's bomb-load was one 4000-pounder, four 1000-pounders, one 500-pounder, target indicators and flares. His only comments in his log book were, "Bombed fires. No opposition on route. Accurate barrage over target." His flight time was 6:45 hours, and his running total to date is pencilled at 404:35 hours.

In a letter home he wrote, "It was a quiet trip except when over the target but we got through without being hit."

After the Stuttgart raid, Fraser was halfway through his third and final tour, with just 10 operations to go.

Two days later Fraser flew a Lancaster to Turnhouse aerodrome just outside Edinburgh to be best man at the wedding of Rhys Jones, an Australian sergeant he befriended at Westcott. After the wedding, Fraser returned overnight on the *Flying Scotsman*. When he reached Oakington he found his name on the battle orders for that night. But later in the day the raid was cancelled, much to his relief as he hadn't slept on the train journey.

Early in March, Fraser took over as temporary commander of 7 Squadron while the squadron leader took a week's leave. During his tenure there were no major raids planned by Bomber Command, but Fraser did manage to 'requisition' a Lancaster on two occasions to fly to Westcott to visit Marie. On both occasions a basic crew would tag along for the jaunt. But Fraser played down the frolics in a letter home, "Being a Wing Commander isn't all fun and games, or beer and skittles, whichever you prefer."

72 Fraser and his crew participated in another raid on Stuttgart on the night of 15/16 March. 863 aircraft took part, including 617 Lancasters, 230 Halifaxes and 16 Mosquitoes. The bomber force flew over France nearly to the Swiss border, before swinging northeast to approach Stuttgart. This delayed the German fighters making contact with the bomber stream, but when the fighters did arrive just before Stuttgart was reached, fierce air battles ensued. Losses were 37 bombers. A further two Lancasters force-landed in Switzerland. Strong winds possibly caused the Pathfinders' marking to fall back before the target, despite the clear weather conditions. Some of the early bombing fell in the centre of Stuttgart, but most fell to the southwest in open country.

Fraser was within 30 minutes of Stuttgart when his starboard-outer motor was shut down and the propeller feathered. This engine, when running, provided auxiliary power to operate the mid-upper turret. Their *H2S* and *Gee* were also unserviceable, so Fraser was forced to abandon the raid. Presumably the bomb-load was carried back home, as no mention otherwise was made in Fraser's log book. The flight still lasted 6:20 hours.

73 Three nights later on 18/19 March, Fraser and his crew bombed Frankfurt. It was a large raid with 846 aircraft taking part, including 620 Lancasters, 209 Halifaxes and 17 Mosquitoes. The high-speed Mosquitoes were slowly becoming a bigger presence on raids as manufacturing allowed. Losses were 22 aircraft. On this occasion the Pathfinders marked the target accurately, leading to heavy bombing across the target from east to west.

Extensive damage was caused to Frankfurt. The local report mentioned

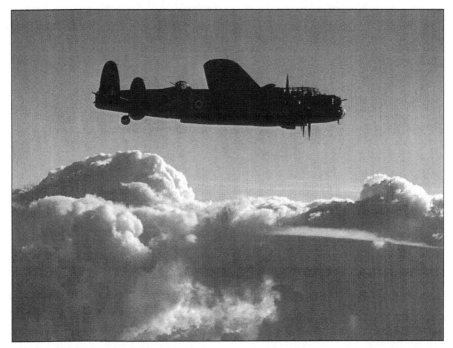

A Lancaster high above the clouds.

5495 houses, 99 industrial firms, 412 small business and 56 public buildings were either destroyed or seriously damaged, and 421 people were killed and 55,500 bombed out.

Fraser only carried one bomb on this raid, a 4000-pounder. He also carried incendiaries, TIs and flares. His *H2S* was again unserviceable. He wrote, "Good trip ... Bombed fires. Flak fairly intense. Many searchlights." Over the target they had the terrifying experience of an incendiary dropped from a bomber higher up hitting their port wing. They were incredibly lucky it didn't ignite or cause them to crash. Their flight time was five hours.

After the Frankfurt raid Fraser and Marie visited the Irelands at Ambleside. But their holiday was cut short when the 7 Squadron commanding officer, Wing Commander Ken Rampling, was lost on a raid to Frankfurt on the night of 22/23 March. Fraser hastily returned to Oakington to take over as temporary commander of the squadron. Sadly, Mrs Ireland would not see Fraser again – this being his last visit to Ambleside.

The new replacement commander, Wing Commander WG Lockhart, took command two days later on 25 March.

74 Fraser's next raid was on Nuremberg on the night of 30/31 March. Sadly, the night would go down in history as the biggest Bomber Command loss of the war. 95 bombers were lost on the Nuremberg raid and one other lost on a minor operation, making a total of 96 lost on the night. 795 aircraft were dispatched, including 572 Lancasters, 214 Halifaxes and nine Mosquitoes.

The German fighter controllers ignored all Bomber Command diversions and concentrated their fighters near two radio beacons which happened to be astride the route to Nuremberg. As the force arrived, the fighters pounced and a fierce battle in the moonlight followed, resulting in 82 bombers being shot down before they reached the target area. By the time of the return flight, most fighters had landed to refuel, so only a

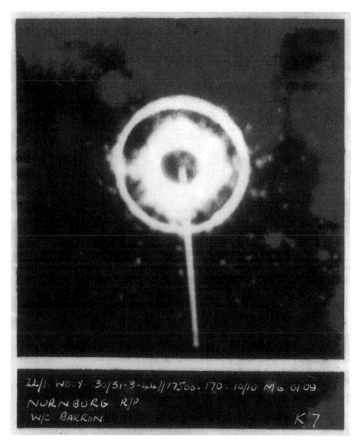

H2S target-marking photograph of raid on Nuremberg, 30/31 March 1944.

few bombers were lost.

Most crews claimed to have bombed the target, but subsequent reconnaissance showed that approximately 120 aircraft bombed Schweinfurt, 50 miles northwest of Nuremberg. The off-target bombing was caused by navigational difficulties in the badly-forecast winds. Two Pathfinders even dropped markers over Schweinfurt.

Fraser's bomb-load was one 4000-pounder, two 1000-pounders and target indicators. He recorded in his log book, "Easy trip … 10/10 [cloud] at target. Detailed as visual marker but retained TIs. 96 a/c [aircraft] lost." Fraser's flight time was 6:30 hours.

Fraser wrote home, "The last one was three nights ago to Nuremberg when we lost a record of 96 of our bombers. It's very funny, but it was the quietest trip I've ever been on. I seem to have the most amazing luck." Fraser usually described his third-tour raids as either an "easy," or "good," or "quiet" trip. So far for Fraser it had been a "piece of cake."

The next day Fraser flew an Oxford to Westcott to spend an hour with Marie, who must have been hugely relieved to see him alive. Like about 750 other airmen on the previous night, Fraser could have been shot down over Germany. He repeated the jaunt to Westcott on 4 April, only this time he stayed over for a night.

Yet again, Fraser landed a Lancaster at Westcott in the middle of a 'fighter affiliation' training exercise on 13 April. The flight just happened to go in that direction!

During April, 7 Squadron split off one flight to form a new squadron. It wasn't replaced, with the remaining two flights each increasing the number of crews from 13 to 14. The split didn't involve Fraser, as he and his crew remained with 7 Squadron.

Softening up for D-Day

The Allied invasion of Normandy by Allied ground forces, *Operation Overlord*, would commence in less than 10 weeks on 6 June 1944. Most of Bomber Command's efforts in recent years had been to weaken the general capacity of Germany. But now Harris' squadrons would be directed in a far more precise manner against targets inland from the invasion beaches. In doing so, Harris' greatest concern was to hit the numerous small targets without causing too many French casualties.

A priority of Bomber Command would be to hit railway targets in France and Belgium with a view to isolating the German forces in Normandy by hampering railway-borne reinforcements. Also planned were raids on military bases, ammunition depots and explosives and armament factories in France and Belgium, and just prior to the invasion, on radio and radar stations and coastal gun batteries. Then there were always roads, fighter-based aerodromes and communication centres to be targeted.

There was one aspect of the coming bombing that bomber crews were unaware of – a massive Allied deception plan would come into operation to persuade the Germans into thinking that the main landing would be in the Pas de Calais area, 150 miles north of Normandy. This meant that for every bomb that was dropped on the railway system leading to Normandy, almost as many bombs needed to be dropped further north.

Bomber Command would share these softening-up duties with the American daytime-operating 8th Air Force, and with the RAF tactical day-bomber and fighter forces. On the few nights when Bomber Command would not be needed for pre-invasion targets, cities in Germany were to be attacked.

Bomber Command would become very successful at bombing small discreet targets in France and Belgium. The use of a master bomber on these raids became standard practice, but their crews often became casualties as they remained flying in the target area throughout the raids.

A Lancaster circles an airfield before landing.

Generally, bomber crews were keen to be involved in the invasion and liberation of Europe, and attacking targets of a more military nature rather than bombing civilians in German cities. They were also relieved that the long winter with its costly raids into Germany was over.

75 Fraser's first operation under the new strategic plan was to act as master bomber for an attack by 171 aircraft on railway marshalling yards at Tergnier in northwest France, on the night of 18/19 April 1944. The force comprised 139 Halifaxes, 24 Lancasters and eight Mosquitoes, of which six Halifaxes were lost. The raid caused 50 railway lines to be severed but most of the bombing fell on housing areas southwest of the railway yards. The number of French civilian casualties was not known.

Fraser wrote in his log book, "Detailed Master of Ceremonies. Bombed from 9500 feet. TIs only. Circled target at 5000 feet and directed attack but main force persisted in dropping bombs to southwest. Dropped own bombs from 4000 feet."

Fraser, as master bomber, then had to put himself and his crew at peril by flying over the target at only 2000 feet to observe the results. He concluded that the raid was a failure. Flight time was four hours.

76 For his next two raids, Fraser was taken off pre-invasion targets and directed back to Germany. The first was to Cologne on the night of 20/21 April. 357 Lancasters and 22 Mosquitoes took part with four Lancasters being lost. This concentrated attack was aimed at areas of Cologne which were north and west of the city centre, and partly industrial in nature. 1861 houses or apartments were destroyed and more than 20,000 damaged. There were 1290 separate fires, and 664 people were killed and 1067 injured. Improved high-explosive bombs penetrated normally safe basement shelters where 80% of the casualties occurred.

Fraser had little to say about the raid. "10/10 cloud over target. Good run on box [*H2S*]. Easy trip." Fraser's flight time was 3:40 hours. He now had only five operations to complete his third and final tour.

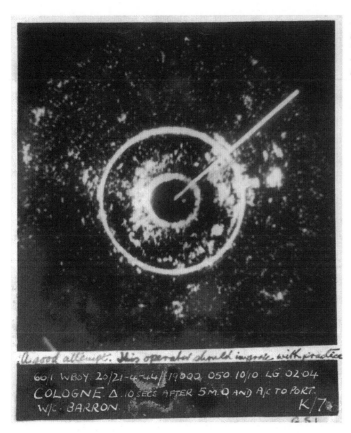

H2S target-marking photograph of raid on Cologne, 20/21 April 1944. Across the photograph is written, "A good attempt. This operator should improve with practice."

77 The second trip to Germany was to Karlsruhe on the night of 24/25 April. 637 aircraft took part – 369 Lancasters, 259 Halifaxes and nine Mosquitoes. Losses were 19 aircraft. Cloud over the target and a strong wind which pushed the Pathfinders too far north botched the raid. Only the northern part of Karlsruhe was seriously damaged with most of the bombs falling outside the city.

Fraser's bomb-load was one 4000-pounder, four 1000-pounders, one 500-pounder and flares. His only comments were, "Target identified. Good run. Moderate accurate flak over target. Quiet trip." His flight time was 5:50 hours.

Fraser's Squadron Commander, Wing Commander WG Lockhart, elected to fly on a raid on the night of 27/28 April to Friedrichshafen. This meant Fraser had to remain behind in command. Lockhart's regular flight engineer was not available for the trip, so Fraser's flight engineer, Lofty Johnson, stood in for him. Sadly, the crew was lost on the night. The loss hit Fraser hard as this was his first regular crew member to be lost on operations.

Fraser was forced to look for a replacement. Meanwhile, Flight Sergeant D Morrison joined Fraser's crew as a temporary replacement.

The loss of Lockhart returned Fraser to overall command of the squadron until a new commander was appointed. Fraser didn't need the added responsibilities, as he wanted to concentrate on his primary roles of bomber captain and master bomber.

On three different occasions during mid to late April, Fraser flew the squadron's Oxford to Westcott to visit Marie. He also visited her on 7 May, the same day of his next operation. Fraser was getting into the habit of either visiting Marie before or just after each raid. Because their relationship had flourished recently, Marie probably needed reassurance that Fraser was safe, as she would read about bomber losses in the daily papers.

78 Fraser's next raid on the night of 7/8 May was back to a pre-invasion target in France. Again, he was appointed master bomber. His crew included a few new faces: Squadron Leader Bob Coldwell, navigator; Squadron Leader John Baker, bomb aimer; Warrant

Officer RR Claridge, wireless operator; Flight Sergeant D Morrison, flight engineer; and Flight Sergeant O Erasmus and Flying Officer Wharton, both air gunners. Squadron Leader John Baker DFC recently joined 7 Squadron as Navigation Leader.

The target was Nantes Airfield, near the coast, just east of Saint Nazaire. 93 Lancasters and six Mosquitoes took part – one Lancaster was lost.

To give an idea of what Fraser's role as master bomber involved: The method of bombing on the night was a *Musical Parramatta* personally directed by Fraser from the cockpit of his Lancaster. The Mosquitoes, using *Oboe*, were to drop green spot flares and red and green TIs (target indicators) from H-8 (zero hour less eight minutes) to H-6. The Illuminators at H-6, flying at 10,000 feet, were to aim white flares at the centre of the TIs. If no TIs were visible, their orders were to release flares using *H2S*, or on a positive visual identification. The master bomber (Fraser), and his deputy master bomber, also in a Lancaster, were to be on target at H-5 at 8-9000 feet, when Fraser was to release additional markers if required. The deputy was to drop additional white TIs as instructed by Fraser. For this raid Fraser's call sign was Free Gift One, and both Fraser and his deputy were ordered to leave the target area at H+6. Zero hour was 03:00 (3am).

Fraser was only meant to be in the target area for about 11 minutes, but being a perfectionist he probably hung around for longer than necessary to ascertain the effect of the bombing. Throughout his time over the target, he would radio instructions to his deputy and direct other participants of the raid.

Fraser was possibly only carrying white TIs on the night. His comments from his log book were, "Dropped white TIs on AP [aiming point]. Directed deputy to do same. Good prang [bombing raid] with plenty of fires and explosions. Opposition hotter than usual." His flight took five hours and his running total was now 450:35 hours on operations.

The results of the raid were encouraging with a concentrated bomb pattern achieved. Air reconnaissance the following day showed 250 bomb craters on the airfield including 30 direct hits on the runways. Three of the four hangars were damaged, two hits were scored on an ammunition dump and three barracks were destroyed.

Using the squadron Oxford, Fraser visited Westcott and Marie the day after the Nantes raid. This was the last time the two would see each other.

At this time Fraser wrote his last-known letter home to his mother and family. One senses from the snippets in the letter, that Fraser was rushed and penned it to satisfy his mother's desire for news.

> England 13 May 1944
> Dear Mum
> Sorry I haven't written for a couple of weeks but I've been very busy.
> We lost our CO [Ken Rampling] on operations a fortnight ago and I've been commanding the squadron since then. The new CO is coming next week and then I hope I won't have so much to do.
> I haven't done much flying since then as this job keeps me going on the ground all day and most of the night. I've done another two or three raids though and have now done 78. I'll be finishing after another six.
> The only night I've really had off in the last two weeks was last Monday night when we had our squadron dance. Marie came up for it and it was a pretty good show.
> Mrs Ireland was expecting me up on leave last week but I couldn't get off, of course. Still, I am hoping to get off in another couple of weeks and I think I'll take a fortnight off to make up for the leave I lost.
> Yesterday I had an aerograph from you, and in it you said that Gordon McLachlan was mining in the Pacific.
> For the last few weeks, we have had very hot weather in this part of the country.
> It has been almost as good as the weather we used to get in New Zealand.
> However, it has started to rain today which is really a good job as it is badly needed.
> Bill [Black] is on a course in London at the moment, but I have heard from him only once in the last six weeks and needless to say, I haven't written to him. I had a letter from Hector which I

must try to answer tonight.

That's all the news this time. I'll try to write again next week.

Love to Dad, Patsy and all the others.

Love from Fraser

In the letter Fraser mentioned that after 78 operations, he still had a further six to complete – a total of 84. This conflicts with the 81 operations allotted to him by his command – 61 plus the 20 from his third tour. Somehow Fraser had managed to extend his tour by a further three operations. Perhaps, being Acting Squadron Leader, Fraser just asserted his authority.

About this time Fraser welcomed Flight Sergeant Derek Wood, his new flight engineer, to the crew.

On 19 May, Fraser and his crew, who had returned from leave, gathered to plan their attack scheduled for that night on the Arnage railway marshalling yards at Le Mans in France, halfway between Paris and the previous target of Nantes.

Through adversity to the stars

79 Preparations for the raid on Le Mans on the night of 19/20 May 1944 were fairly relaxed for Fraser and his crew. They knew the target required only shallow penetration across French territory and the German defences over the target were expected to be light. They also knew that any fighter opposition would be split between half a dozen different targets, including Tours, Amiens, Orléans and Boulogne.

Fraser had already been appointed master bomber for the raid and Squadron Leader Johnny Dennis DSO, DFC, his deputy. Following their late-afternoon briefing the crew enjoyed a pre-flight meal and took time out to write letters, listen to music, read and chat amongst themselves. After 9pm they gathered in their locker rooms to change into warm flying gear. After checking equipment and collecting their

A Lancaster en route to fortress Europe.

parachutes, they gathered around a squadron truck ready to be delivered to their aircraft.

After being dropped alongside their Lancaster, ND845, *C for Charlie*, the same aircraft Fraser used on the Nantes raid, they met with the ground crew and discussed any problems they might have experienced in preparing the aircraft.

The crew for the night was Fraser's regular crew with the addition of Baker and Wood. The seven were: Squadron Leaders Bob Coldwell DSO, DFM and John Baker DSO, DFC, Pilot Officer Albert Price, Flying Officers Jack Walters DFC and Bob Weatherall DFM, Flight Sergeant Derek Wood, and Warrant Officer Joe Lamonby.

Finally, as take-off time approached, cigarettes were extinguished and a last pee taken on the bomber's tail wheel, and the men climbed aboard and settled into their positions, connecting to the intercom and making themselves comfortable. Fraser then checked with each crewman over the intercom and, along with Derek Wood, went through the engine

Year: 1944		Aircraft.		Pilot, or 1st Pilot.	2nd Pilot, Pupil, or Passenger.	Duty (Including Results and Remarks).
month	date	Type.	No.			
—	—	—	—	—	—	— Totals Brought Forward
Summary for	Apr:				Lancaster	
Unit	7 Sqadrn				Oxford	
Date	1/5/44				3.	
Signature	J Barron					
May	7	Oxford	769	Self		To Westcott and Return
May	7	Lancaster III	845	Self	S/Ldr. Coldwell S/Ldr. Baker W/O. Claridge H/Sgt. Morrison F/Sgt. Eastwood F/O. Wharton	78. Raid on Nantes Airfield. Master Bomber. Dropped T.I.s while on A/P. Directed Deputy to do same. Good prang with plenty of fires and explosions. Opposition better than usual
May	14	Lancaster III	389	Self	Sgt. Derrick	To Westcott and Return
May	19	LANCASTER III		SELF	S/LDR. COLDWELL S/LDR. BAKER P/O. PRICE F/O. WALTERS F/S. WOOD. F/O. WEATHERALL. W/O. LAMONBY.	79. RAID ON LE MANS. MARSHALLING YARDS.
		SUMMARY FOR :-	MAY 1944			
		UNIT:-	No. 7 SQDN.			LANCASTER III.
		DATE:-	29.5.44			
		SIGNATURE:-	Baker S/L			

The last entries in Fraser's log book. Details of the 19/20 May raid were entered by the squadron leader.

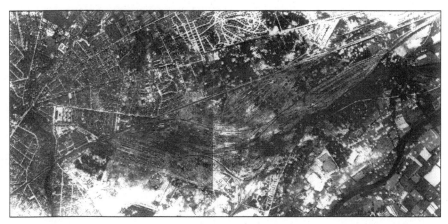

Reconnaissance photograph montage of Arnage railway marshalling yards at Le Mans, showing the extensive damage caused by raids on 19/20 and 22/23 May 1944.

start-up drills. When all four engines were running smoothly and final checks completed, Fraser waved for the chocks to be removed. The Lancaster moved slowly out of its dispersal pan onto the taxiway and, after a final thumbs up from the ground crew, moved towards the holding point and runway.

A quick call was made to the crew, "All set for take off?" After their responses and final green light from the runway controller, Fraser commenced his take-off run. This was always an anxious time because of the volatile bomb-load and high-octane fuel aboard. Once airborne, the undercarriage was raised and a gentle climb started.

The force heading to Le Mans, and the Arnage marshalling yards on the south side, comprised 112 Lancasters and four Mosquitoes, all from 3 and 8 Groups. Six of the Lancasters were dispatched by 7 Squadron. They skirted to the west of London, crossed Brighton on the Sussex coast and headed due south, passing within six miles of heavy defences at Le Havre. From here they headed directly to the target.

The four Mosquitoes, two from each of 105 and 109 Squadrons, were due to mark the aiming point at Arnage using *Oboe* at H-8 to H-7. Two Mosquitoes had equipment failure, but the remaining two – Squadron Leader WW Blessing of 105 and Squadron Leader RC Cobbe of 109 – accurately marked the aiming point on time with three red and three green TIs from 30,000 feet.

Fraser then arrived in the target area on time with Illuminators, but because of thick cloud cover over the target, was forced to release his flares using *H2S*. He was not happy with this, realising that if the Main Force remained at 12,000 feet, they would see neither the flares nor the TIs because of the thick cloud cover sitting between 8000 and 10,000 feet. Determined to make the raid a success, he descended below the cloud and marked the aiming point with yellow TIs, a different colour from the earlier-released TIs. He also assessed the yellow TIs were falling about 200 yards north of the target – such was the accuracy of his crew's efforts.

While Fraser was placing the new markers, he called the Main Force over his radio, telling them to descend below the cloud barrier and aim their bombs just to the south of the centre of the yellow TIs. His instructions were heard by most of the bombers. Some remained above the cloud barrier and later claimed that "excessive chat" by crews over the assigned radio frequency made the master bomber's new orders unreadable.

Fraser then circled the target area. The markers soon became less distinct and the main attack, which started bombing accurately, became more scattered. As a last resort, Fraser called on his deputy, Squadron Leader Johnny Dennis, to lay on some of his white TIs to refocus the attack. This was done precisely. Fraser and Johnny were now both circling the target at 4000 feet or lower, watching the bomb detonations on the ground.

At this time, observers in other aircraft noticed light tracer flak coming from the target area and something falling from the sky. It was the two Lancasters crashing, killing both crews instantly. Whether one of the two Lancasters was hit by the flak and collided with the other, or one tried to evade the flak and hit the other, we will never know. No further transmissions were received from either aircraft.

It was later established that Fraser's Lancaster crashed into the Renault works, close to the aiming point. Johnny's crashed elsewhere in Le Mans.

A third Lancaster was also lost on the raid. In a strange twist of fate, the bomb aimer on board this aircraft was Pilot Officer Rhys Jones, whom Fraser was best man for. Rhys is buried in the same cemetery as Fraser.

About six hours after takeoff, 7 Squadron were expecting their crews to arrive home at Oakington. Only four of the original six aircraft landed. Ground crews became increasingly anxious while they scanned the sky. Finally, knowing that the aircraft could no longer be airborne because of available fuel, they returned to the warmth of the buildings.

FTR – 'failed to return,' was posted against Fraser's name on the blackboard in the Operations Room. It was a great shock. The impossible had happened. It was unthinkable to all that Fraser would be lost. He was immortal, indestructible, he always came back. Bad luck happened to others – not to Fraser.

The next morning Wing Commander RW Cox assumed command of 7 Squadron. Oakington was a sad place over the following days. The Waafs in the mess seemed to be the most upset. But there was a war on. Soon the squadron lost further crews on subsequent raids and the raid on Le Mans largely became just another operation.

When Marie received the bad news, she was grief-stricken. But it was not unexpected, Fraser had been playing a game of chance and his number had finally come up.

James Barron, Fraser's father, received the telegram that all parents of servicemen dread. It arrived on 22 May. It read, "Regret to inform you

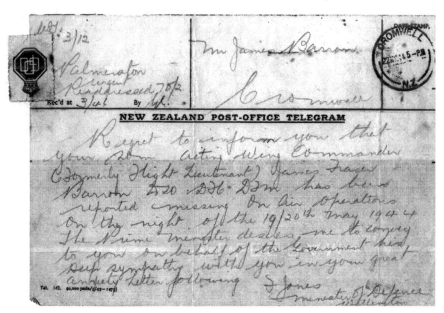

Hand-written telegram received by Mr James Barron informing him of his son's death.

Original shared grave of Fraser Barron and Flight Sergeant Derek Wood, Le Mans. Beside them is Rhys Jones, killed during the same raid. The bodies were later reinterred in the Commonwealth War Graves section of the Le Mans West Cemetery (Cimetière de l'Ouest).

that your son Acting Wing Commander (formerly Flight Lieutenant) James Fraser Barron DSO, DFC, DFM, has been reported missing on air operations on the night of 19/20th May 1944."

Initially, both the Barron family in New Zealand, and Marie and close friends in England, including the Irelands, hoped Fraser parachuted to safety and was taken prisoner, or even escaped to Spain. The waiting must have been desperate.

Three weeks later the Barrons received another telegram. They hoped it contained good news about their son, but the telegram acknowledged a further award for Fraser. It was a second award of the Distinguished Service Order, a Bar to Fraser's DSO, in recognition of his gallantry and skill as master bomber on the Nantes airfield attack. The Official Citation, dated 16 June 1944, not only sums up Fraser's efforts on the night, but also his whole bombing career spread over three years and 79 operations. "One night in May, 1944, Wing Commander Barron participated in an attack on an airfield at Nantes. By his appreciation of the responsibilities entrusted to him and the skill and precision with which he executed his attack, Wing Commander Barron contributed in a large measure to the successes achieved. Since being awarded the DSO he has taken part in many attacks on dangerous and difficult targets. He is an outstanding

Wt. 25617/P1434 100,000 Pads 9/43 H.P. 51-7341

R.A.F. Form 1924   **POSTAGRAM.**   Originator's Reference Number:—
BC/S.23191/P.

To: A/W/C J. F. Barron, DSO,DFC,DFM.(NZ.401749),   Date:—
No. 7 Squadron,
R.A.F. Station, OAKINGTON.   31st May, 1944.

From: The Commander-in-Chief, Bomber Command.

My warmest congratulations on the award of your first Bar to the Distinguished Service Order.

A.J. Harris
Air Chief Marshal.

Originator's
Signature   Time of
Origin

The bizarre congratulatory postagram sent by Harris to Fraser, 10 days after Fraser was killed.

captain whose example of skill, bravery and determination has impressed all."

Fraser's mother attended a private audience of the Governor General, Sir Bernard Freyberg VC, in Dunedin, 27 February 1948, to receive the decoration on behalf of her son.

Today, Fraser is buried in the small Le Mans West Cemetery, in the northwest of Le Mans, west of the River Sarthe. With him are Derek Wood, Bob Coldwell and John Baker. Bob Weatherall is buried alongside other Canadians in Normandy, and Albert Price, Jack Walters and Joe Lamonby have no known graves, so are commemorated on the Runnymede Memorial, in Surrey.

Per ardua ad astra – through adversity to the stars.

Award of the Bar to the Distinguished Service Order to
Wing Commander James Fraser Barron, D.S.O., D.F.C. and Bar,
D.F.M., Royal New Zealand Air Force - 1944.

_____

Copy of official citation.

"One night in May, 1944, Wing Commander Barron
participated in an attack on an airfield at Nantes. By
his appreciation of the responsibilities entrusted to
him and the skill and precision with which he executed
his attack, Wing Commander Barron contributed in a large
measure to the successes achieved. Since being awarded
the D.S.O. he has taken part in many attacks on dangerous
and difficult targets. He is an outstanding captain whose
example of skill and bravery and determination has impressed
all."

_____

Copy of the Official Citation for Fraser's Bar to the DSO.

Obverse and reverse views of Fraser Barron's Memorial Cross sent to Mrs Barron after the war.

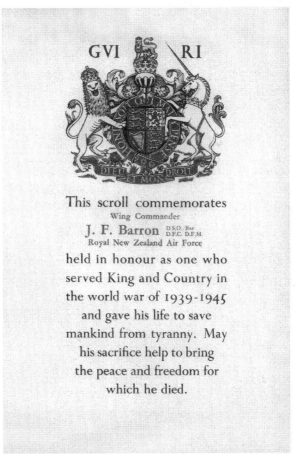

Death Scroll of Wing Commander Fraser Barron.

GVI RI

This scroll commemorates
Wing Commander
J. F. Barron D.S.O./Bar D.F.C. D.F.M.
Royal New Zealand Air Force
held in honour as one who
served King and Country in
the world war of 1939-1945
and gave his life to save
mankind from tyranny. May
his sacrifice help to bring
the peace and freedom for
which he died.